THE STORY THAT CHOOSES US

THE GOSPEL AND OUR CULTURE SERIES

A series to foster the missional encounter of the gospel
with North American culture

John R. Franke
SERIES EDITOR

•   •

Volumes Published to Date

The Story That Chooses Us

A Tapestry of Missional Vision

George R. Hunsberger

WILLIAM B. EERDMANS PUBLISHING COMPANY

GRAND RAPIDS, MICHIGAN / CAMBRIDGE, U.K.

Wm. B. Eerdmans Publishing Co.

2140 Oak Industrial Drive N.E., Grand Rapids, Michigan 49505 /
P.O. Box 163, Cambridge CB3 9PU U.K.

Printed in the United States of America

21 20 19 18 17 16 15   7 6 5 4 3 2 1

Library of Congress Cataloging-in-Publication Data

Hunsberger, George R.

The story that chooses us: a tapestry of missional vision / George R. Hunsberger.

pages   cm

ISBN 978-0-8028-7219-7 (pbk.: alk. paper)

1. Missions. 2. Mission of the church. 3. Newbigin, Lesslie.

4. Storytelling — Religious aspects — Christianity.   I. Title.

BV2035.H86   2015

266 — dc23

2014042858

www.eerdmans.com

Contents

Acknowledgments

The essays in this volume were previously published in journals and books as indicated below. They have undergone very minor revisions, and permission has been granted for their reprinting here.

Gospel — The Story That Chooses Us
  "Foreword — The Story That Chooses Us," in *StormFront: The Good News of God,* by James V. Brownson, Inagrace T. Dietterich, Barry A. Harvey, and Charles C. West (Grand Rapids: Eerdmans, 2003), pp. vi-xii. Revised for use in the present volume.

Challenge — The Newbigin Gauntlet
  "The Newbigin Gauntlet: Developing a Domestic Missiology for North America," *Missiology: An International Review* 19, no. 4 (1991): 391-408. Reprinted in *The Church between Gospel and Culture,* ed. George R. Hunsberger and Craig Van Gelder (Grand Rapids: Eerdmans, 1996), pp. 3-25.

Dilemma — A Vendor-Shaped Church
  "Sizing up the Shape of the Church," *Reformed Review* 47, no. 2 (Winter 1994): 133-44. Reprinted in *The Church between Gospel and Culture,* ed. George R. Hunsberger and Craig Van Gelder (Grand Rapids: Eerdmans, 1996), pp. 333-46.

Calling — Representing the Reign of God
  "Missional Vocation: Called and Sent to Represent the Reign of God," in

Acknowledgments

Missional Church: A Vision for the Sending of the Church in North America, by Darrell L. Guder (ed.), Lois Y. Barrett, Inagrace T. Dietterich, George R. Hunsberger, Alan J. Roxburgh, and Craig Van Gelder (Grand Rapids: Eerdmans, 1998), pp. 77-109.

Community — Truly and True
"The Church in the Postmodern Transition," in *A Scandalous Prophet: The Way of Mission after Newbigin,* ed. Thomas F. Foust, George R. Hunsberger, J. Andrew Kirk, and Werner Ustorf (Grand Rapids: Eerdmans, 2002), pp. 95-106.

Warrant — Announcing the Reign of God
"Is There Biblical Warrant for Evangelism?" *Interpretation* 48, no. 2 (April 1994): 131-44. Reprinted in *The Study of Evangelism: Exploring a Missional Practice of the Church,* ed. Paul W. Chilcote and Laceye C. Warner (Grand Rapids: Eerdmans, 2008), pp. 59-72.

Encounter — Sitting on Both Sides
"Acquiring the Posture of a Missionary Church," *Insights* 108, no. 2 (Fall 1993): 19-26. Reprinted in *The Church between Gospel and Culture,* ed. George R. Hunsberger and Craig Van Gelder (Grand Rapids: Eerdmans, 1996), pp. 289-97; reprinted in abridged form in *Collision Crossroads: The Intersection of Modern Western Culture with the Christian Gospel,* ed. John Flett (Auckland, New Zealand: The DeepSight Trust, 1998).

Place — Discerning Local Vocation
"Discerning Missional Vocation," in *Treasure in Clay Jars: Patterns in Missional Faithfulness,* by Lois Y. Barrett et al. (Grand Rapids: Eerdmans, 2004), pp. 33-58.

Posture — Renewing a Public Voice
"The Missional Voice and Posture of Public Theologizing," *Missiology: An International Review* 34, no. 1 (January 2006): 15-28.

Formation — Cultivating Ways of Christ
"Cultivating Ways of Christ for People in the Postmodern Transition: Resources in the Vision of Lesslie Newbigin," *Journal for Preachers* 22, no. 1 (1998): 12-18. Reprinted as "Renewing Faith During the Postmodern Transition," in *TransMission* (Tribute to Lesslie Newbigin, 1998): 10-

13, and in four installments as "Cultivating Ways of Christ in the Post-modern Transition: Resources for Pastoral Leaders," in *The Gospel and Our Culture Newsletter* 11, no. 1 (March 1999): 3; 11, no. 2 (June 1999): 3; 11, no. 3 (September 1999): 3; and 11, no. 4 (December 1999): 3.

Preface

Over the last couple of decades, there have been frequent occasions to put into writing some facet or other of what I believed to be at stake for the church's recovery of its missional identity and practice. Each occasion arose in light of some particular problematic in the church or its context. Each called for a response along particular lines, developing particular themes. Each response was nourished by the grace of collegial conversation with others engaging similar issues.

It wasn't always evident to me that, in the course of time, those more focused articles and chapters, when gathered together, comprise something of a web of vision, a sweep of missional perspective for our present time and place. Perhaps *tapestry* is a better word. In the essays chosen and re-presented in this volume, there are a number of themes that gently recur and echo throughout, weaving together a tapestry of missional-ecclesial vision.

For readers who have read some of these essays before, the intention is that the present volume may offer a sense of the connections between them and their overall scope when they are read together in this way. It is hoped that the renewed titles for the essays will be suggestive toward that end, and that the order in which they are placed may further illustrate the way they build on each other.

This means, of course, that the essays are not simply placed in chronological order. It is important, however, for the reader to keep in mind *when* each essay was written in order to be able to interpret and weigh what is being said, and how, and why. So, at the beginning of each chapter, the date of original publication is prominently noted. (Other de-

tails of original and subsequent publication are available on the Acknowl-
edgments page.)

I offer the essays in this present volume with a deep sense of gratitude for the host of companions who have nourished me and nourished the
vision these essays represent — family (wife, parents, children, grandchil-
dren, and more), congregations of which I have been a part, colleagues in
the missiological guild, companions in the college and seminary faculties
where I have taught (Belhaven and Western Theological Seminary), editors
and their associates who make publication possible and keep it responsible.
Perhaps most of all, I have been immeasurably enriched over many years by
association with the hundreds — thousands — of companions in the Gospel and Our Culture Network. In particular, I am indebted to those GOCN
companions with whom I was privileged to be engaged in research and
writing, especially the teams in whose company two of these essays were
framed and expressed (the chapters on "Calling" and "Place").

As are so many of us, I am indebted to the life and thought of Lesslie
Newbigin, whose influence sparked the origin of the GOCN and whose
thinking has pervaded the subsequent conversations. While Newbigin's
thought is most directly engaged in the two chapters which are deliberate expositions of his thinking (the first, "Challenge," and the last, "Formation"), his influence will be readily observable throughout.

GOSPEL

The Story That Chooses Us

2003

> Galadriel: *The world is changed. I feel it in the water. I feel it in the earth. I smell it in the air. Much that once was, is lost, for none now live who remember it.*
>
> J. R. R. Tolkien, *The Fellowship of the Ring*

The world changes. There are times when we know that. Once familiar story-lines take a sharp turn this way or that or vanish altogether. Fragments of memory grow pale. Patchwork imaginings stir only the faintest of hopes that some story may again find the world and nourish it back to life.

But which story? And which telling of it? Maybe it has been more true of other times than we have thought, but in our time, at least, the contending parables multiply. No longer does a single story hold it all together. Each of us is under a funny kind of obligation to find our own, make up our own, claim our own.

All the while, Christian storytellers live in the grip of an ancient-present story centered in the life, death, and resurrection of Jesus. They have found that this story has read them inside and out, it has laid bare their motives and the movements of their spirits. It has captured them into its still-unfolding drama. They know the experience of Frodo — the Hobbit hero of J. R. R. Tolkien's classic, now cinematized, trilogy — who without willing it or wanting it came into possession of a ring whose own adventure changed everything in the path of his life. Not only had the ring chosen Frodo. The responsibility to see the ring to the fires of Mordor for its destruction had chosen him as well. And the company who shared "this sort of . . . mission . . . quest . . . thing" (to quote Frodo's companion, Pippin) was implicated in the choosing.

The job of telling "gospel" — the good news of God — is always a fresh challenge that requires the teller to have ears to hear and eyes to see. Many of the older ways the story has been told are ready at hand, ways shaped by other times and places that demanded certain tones and accents if the story was to be heard in a way that was true to its first telling. But as the Christian story gets told over and over in a given place, it can as easily as not be overpowered by other claims and visions that absorb it into their own agendas. So it has been in the North American scene. Gradually, many of us have been driven back to our origins with ears and eyes eager to see, to hear, to know that first story. And we are stirred to render it fresh for this new time and place.

Increasingly, Christians today are learning to testify that the good news of God has captured them. Whether or not they ever thought otherwise, they know that the significant thing is not that they chose to hold to the story for some personal benefit, real or imagined. Rather, they know the story came as the news of God that required the allegiance of their lives. It has worked its ever-more-compelling power on them to put them to this way, this quest, this mission. It is this that makes them the church.

Several years ago, a group of four authors took up a challenge presented to them by companions in the Gospel and Our Culture Network.[1] They set out to achieve what they came to call "a faithful and compelling performance of the gospel." They wanted to say as clearly and directly as possible what they heard to be the good news of God, as told in the Christian Scriptures and as it bears on the peculiar ways of life of today's North Americans.[2]

The word "performance" has a very particular meaning when used this way. It is not used in the sense of entertainment. Rather, it is used in reference to the way any language functions. A performance of a language is not the language itself, with all its established conventions of grammar, fields of meaning, etc. It is an act of speech uttered by someone in that language. Such an utterance corresponds to the conventions of the language enough to be understood by others who know the language, and thus it

---

1. The group included Jim Brownson, Inagrace Dietterich, Barry Harvey, and Charles West.

2. The fruit of their work was the book *StormFront: The Good News of God*, by James V. Brownson et al. (Grand Rapids: Eerdmans, 2003).

communicates meaning. But it is an utterance distinct to the user at a particular moment, an example of the use of the language.

Let me illustrate from the days when my children were learning to understand and speak English. My daughter Lauren, when she was very young, stirred us to laughter one day with one of her attempts to speak our common language. She had obviously observed adult speech "performances" and had detected from them the way English works. Hearing others express in one way or another something like, "That's a good idea," and learning which moments might bring forth such an expression, she decided to try it out for herself. The right moment arrived, and she made the attempt: "That could be a idea!" Her performance of the language was a true and fitting use of it, while just odd enough in the particulars to bring us a good laugh. We still chuckle decades later when we remember that early performance.

StormFront is a performance of the gospel of God. The first record we have of that gospel, of course, are the earliest documents of the Christian tradition. Those documents of the New Testament have a privileged place for setting the grammar, establishing the language of the story, and thereby setting in place the kinds of understanding appropriate to it. The reiteration of the news in *StormFront* is a performance tested by its correspondence to those Scriptures. It is also to be tested by how well it hears and reads their nuances in a way that connects with the deep reverberations of the human spirit in the soul of today's North America.

The written, verbal performance of good news presented in that book is offered in clear recognition that the daily lived performance by vibrant communities of Christ is the most fundamental testament to the gospel's force and power. The lived performance is the more compelling and crucial. It is that which will tell what is live-able about this ancient-present story. In one sense, the book simply attempts to give articulation to what is important in those lived performances that are all around us.

On the other hand, the book has something important to say to those Christian communities. It encourages them to give greater attention to their responsibility to give the good news of God its lived expression. The authors offer them a fresh and challenging vision, gleaned from the Scriptures and played against the backdrop of the way our culture has tended to tame and distort the gospel. They argue for the renewing capacity of a fresh, sensitive hearing of the gospel and offer it to encourage the church to make faithfulness to the gospel its greatest aim.

When the authors tell us what the good news of God is, it is obvious that to them this is a "story that chooses us," much as Frodo found himself to be chosen. The threads of their storyline are woven in this direction.

We live in an ever-swirling *storm*.

> *Gandalf [to a despairing Frodo]:* There is more at work in this world than the force of Evil. Bilbo was meant to have the Ring, in which case you also were meant to have it. And that is an encouraging thought.

The coming reign of God, now entered into our affairs in the person of Jesus, sets in motion the collision of systems of rule and authority. It is along such a storm front as this that the church finds itself called into being and implicated on the side of what God is still steadily and faithfully intending for the world, a world in which there is "more at work than the force of evil." And that is an encouraging thought.

We live in a contest of *allegiance*.

> *Frodo:* I wish the ring had never come to me. I wish none of this had happened.
>
> *Gandalf:* So do all who live to see such times. But that is not for them to decide. All we have to decide is what to do with the time that is given to us.

Decision. That is the critical matter put before everyone we meet in the Gospels when they come face to face with Jesus. Not a decision about what might be in one's rational self-interest. But a decision about what now must be done "with the time that is given to us."

We live in a life and death *communion*.

> *Aragorn:* The same blood flows in my veins. The same weakness.
>
> *Arwen:* Your time will come. You will face the same evil, and you will defeat it.

The ordinary path of life for Christ-followers is one of deep inner rootedness in the life and death of Jesus. It is the good news of God that we are welcomed into the dying and rising of Jesus, by which he faced the evil and defeated even the final enemy, death. That sharing in Christ is what carves out the shape of the calling, the mission, the sending of the church.

4

We live at the intersection of *powers.*

> *Frodo [speaking about Gollum]:* It's a pity Bilbo didn't kill him when he had the chance.
>
> *Gandalf:* Pity? It was pity that stayed Bilbo's hand. Many that deserve life receive death and many that deserve death do not receive it. Can you give that to them?

Subtle or not so subtle, direct or indirect, overt or covered with layers of pretense, the powers of our world represent profound patterns of resistance to the power of God, coming as it has in the form of a cross. Cross-bearing resistance comes in the form of pity, not vengeance; mercy, not violence; life-giving in place of death-dealing.

We live in a crucible of *practices.*

> *Galadriel:* The Quest stands upon the edge of a knife. Stray but a little, and it will fail, to the ruin of all. Yet hope remains while the Company is true.

Christian practices, churchly practices, are the implication of all this for the life of the church. But not merely practices in the sense of organizational activities. Rather, radical, even subversive, practices are called for, practices that Jesus anticipates in what have been called the Beatitudes. "Stray but a little. . . . Hope remains while the Company is true."

Is this a faithful performance of the gospel? I believe it is. Faithfulness is about hearing, feeling, knowing what was said at the outset that sets the path for what is rightly called Christian. It is always an exercise in community, wrestling to say the gospel with a common voice, as these four authors have done. It has been their experience that their own different takes on the gospel have pushed them each to keep that faith more fully — not captivated by a current trend, nor pretending that they can do anything other than give a reading, a rendering in this time and place, with the mental and language tools our culture gives us, of what was originally announced as the good news. This is no search for some "pure gospel unadulterated by any cultural accretions" — which, as Lesslie Newbigin has had to remind so many of us in the West, is in any case an illusion.[3] Rather, it is a search for a careful and powerful way of putting this story for this generation.

---

3. Lesslie Newbigin, *Foolishness to the Greeks: The Gospel and Western Culture* (Grand Rapids: Eerdmans, 1986), p. 4.

2014

It is this sort of good news that implicates us to give it performance after performance after performance. At the center of the biblical narrations that together "render accessible to us the character, actions, and purposes of God"[4] lies this news that the meaning of the world's life has been revealed most fully now in Jesus Christ and the world's future in the purposes of God is established ("The reign of God is at hand!"). The call we hear from Jesus carries us right into this story, and sets us into its moving path, going to the ends of the earth and to the end of time. Just as for Frodo the responsibility to see the ring to its destruction in the fires of Mordor had *chosen him,* so has this good news *chosen us* into a company, a fellowship, that lives in faithful investment in "this sort of . . . mission . . . quest . . . thing." (Pippin speaks so powerfully, even if haltingly!)

Newbigin saw this to be at the core of Christian identity. From the earliest of his writings to the latest, he encouraged a revolution in the way we recognize our 'election' by God, our conversion to be followers of Christ. He continually stressed what he called "the missionary significance of the biblical doctrine of election" as essential for a mission theology suited to the present moment. When mission, and even belief, are questioned, he found no more essential rationale for either than in this way of understanding. We are not chosen for special privilege, but for special responsibility. We are chosen to bear the witness of the Spirit to all the world.

In due course, his understanding of the missionary significance of election will be further elaborated. For now, we might simply listen to how absolutely personal this gets for Newbigin, and how thoroughly orienting this vision is for him. Here is bedrock, for him:

> The Christian mission is thus to act out in the whole life of the whole world the confession that Jesus is Lord of all. . . . I would distort the truth if I simply spoke of this confession as being mine alone. I make this confession only because *I have been laid hold of by Another* and commissioned to do so. It is not primarily or essentially my decision. By ways that are mysterious to me, that I can only faintly trace, *I have been laid hold of by one greater than I* and led into a place where I must make this confession and where I find no way of making sense of my own life or the life of the world except through being an obedient disciple of Jesus. . . .

4. Newbigin, *Foolishness to the Greeks,* p. 59.

When I am questioned about my right to preach Jesus as Lord among the nations, I can only reply that *I am a simple servant* of one whom God has chosen and sent for the sake of all — Jesus Christ.[5]

In the essays that follow, I share my own testament that I also "have been laid hold of by Another."

5. Lesslie Newbigin, *The Open Secret: An Introduction to the Theology of Mission*, rev. ed. (Grand Rapids: Eerdmans, 1995), pp. 17-18 (emphasis mine).

CHALLENGE

The Newbigin Gauntlet

1991

At Lausanne II, the 1989 gathering of evangelical missionary forces in Manila, time was reserved in the schedule for national gatherings. In those meetings, people from — or working in — each country met to pray, evaluate, share, and strategize regarding the evangelizing task facing the church in that place. In every gathering, that is, except one. The meetings of the US delegates were noteworthy because their focus was not on evangelizing their country but on continuing to mobilize churches in the United States for evangelizing the other countries of the world. The US participants did not see their country as a field for mission, but only as a launching pad for missionizing the "elsewheres" of the world.[1]

The situation is not much better within ecumenical mainline Protestant denominations. For all the talk about "reciprocal mission" or "mission in reverse," the typical North American Protestant church would simply laugh if it were suggested that an African or Asian be called to be the founding pastor/evangelist for a project to plant a new church in an area inhabited by white middle-class folks. We still send white missionaries to plant churches among nonwhite peoples elsewhere in the world, but we cannot conceive of the need for missionaries from other places and cultures to do that here. We fail to see the need for anyone else to help us, not even with the very aspects of the work of the churches that have become most vexing for us (e.g., evangelism). We welcome colleagues from elsewhere as informants on their part of the world. Perhaps we will allow them

1. See Craig Van Gelder, "Evangelicals and Lausanne II: What Happened to a 'Contextual' Gospel?" *The Gospel and Our Culture Newsletter* 2, no. 1 (1990): 5-6.

8

to give a measure of critique from the perspective of their culture. Almost by definition, however, we Americans are "not in need" of missionaries to come help us.

These dynamics betray a mindset that lies at the root of what must be called a glaring gap in American missiology. We have failed to give clear-cut attention to the development of a domestic, contextual missiology for our own North American setting. In its place has grown an implicit, functional missiology suffering from a lack of scrutiny. In most of our churches, ask what people think about "mission," and immediately you get responses about "people over there" in faraway places across the globe, people who have "little or no knowledge" about Christ, among whom our missionaries are working to bring the light of the gospel. Shift the focus by saying, "No, I mean local mission right here." Now what you hear about are benevolent projects for helping the poor and disadvantaged. Again you say, "But what about evangelizing your own community?" Then the conversation shifts to the ways the church is seeking to attract, gain, and retain new members.

"Over there, helping the poor, recruiting members" — these have become the operational missiologies of our churches. And they are not just uninformed notions of laypeople. They are fueled and undergirded by the guidance implicit in the language of missiological institutions and movements. The fund-raising dimensions of denominational and independent global mission agencies transmute what should be occasions for mission education in our churches into mere mission promotion designed to sustain extensive logistic superstructures. The tendency toward social-ethical preaching in our pulpits (whether emphasizing public justice or private moralities) combines with the basic (if fading) American value that every person has a right to material well-being to produce a posture of benevolence toward the poor. The American mystique of growthism makes growing the church larger an end more important than representing the gospel of the reign of God.

Each of these phrases has a measure of validity. But even when taken all together, global mission support (i.e., a large missionary budget), benevolence toward the poor (building houses and supplying food), and church growth efforts (parking lots and visitation programs) form an inadequate notion of a congregation's mission. Its inadequacy shows up in several ways. In the first place, all three facets of the complex enjoy a strong dependence upon root American values (the same values by which we design our economy, gauge national progress, wage war, etc.). We have the attitude that if we *can* do something, we *should* do it. Personal freedom is the greatest good. Material well-being belongs to free people. Growth and success prove that these essential values are right.

While this analysis might suggest that what we have here is, in fact, a very contextualized, domestic missiology — which I have said we lack — I contend that it is not so domestic as it is domesticated. It has arisen comfortably from a set of cultural values that have uncritically been allowed to shape the scope of mission for us.

A second inadequacy follows on the heels of that one. Inherent in the American mythology is a sense that individual freedom — the fundamental myth — is substantiated as a proper foundation for the social order by a supporting myth, material success. The pragmatism, benevolence, and success dimensions of the functional missiology I have been describing function in our congregations in a way similar to their operation in the larger culture, as confirmation and therefore as gauge. If our church grows, the rightness of our faith is somehow verified. We help the poor, but of course we expect to see the proper result, namely, that the poor will then get themselves back on their feet. We support global efforts as long as we see the payoff. The consequence is that these three dynamics of mission function more to serve the self-assurance and self-confidence of the congregation than they serve the world in which the congregation lives or the reign of God that it represents. We feel better when we do these things, and especially when they are done successfully. At bottom, we feel better because we are able to feel OK about ourselves.

The greatest sign of the inadequacy of this reigning missiology is its lack of theological depth, or even theological character. Biblical rationales can always be marshaled, of course. But the fruit of global missiological reflection has scarcely been brought to bear on the need for an operative congregational missiology larger than the present truncated versions. These versions touch so superficially upon the missionary calling of the church that the church in America has become increasingly anemic. As a result, our congregations flounder under the influence of false myths and ultimately unmissionary thinking.

It is to such issues as these that the most recent writings of Lesslie Newbigin have spoken. In effect, he has thrown down the gauntlet, challenging the churches of the West to look to our own contexts as missionary settings and to be as rigorous about what that must mean for our own missionary life as we have been about mission done elsewhere. He was not the first to see the crisis, nor was he the first to ask about the nature of "the missionary encounter of the gospel with Western culture." But in many ways he has become a potent catalyst for focusing our attention on what must become a primary agenda for Western churches. Newbigin's return in the mid-1970s to England, his native land, provided the occasion for him to draw upon the wealth of missionary perspective and statesmanship that had been his contribution within global missiological conversations for several decades. The fruit of that worldwide dialogue fueled his challenge to the churches of the United Kingdom in *The Other Side of 1984* (1983). His way of putting the agenda was sharpened as it was brought more directly to American attention with the publication of *Foolishness to the Greeks* (1986). In *The Gospel in a Pluralist Society* (1989), the essential agenda called for in the earlier books has been further explored along a number of fronts, including especially the development of what might be called a postmodern apologetic to undergird believing and testifying, and the recovery of what it means to be a missionary congregation that serves as the hermeneutic of the gospel.[2]

If Newbigin has thrown down the gauntlet (in the medieval-glove sense of that word), he has accompanied that challenge with an indication of the nature of the gauntlet (in its other meaning) that we are forced to run. His description (particularly in *Foolishness to the Greeks*) of what he sees to be a rudimentary facet of Western culture — namely, the dichotomy that has come to exist between appropriately public "facts" and essentially private "values" — provides clues for understanding a kind of daily gauntlet each of us navigates, believers in Christ no less than other people in the culture. For the church, the effect of the dichotomy strikes at the heart of our self-understandings. The church's former privileged position in Western societies under a Christendom model is now gone, and it will not be regained. The church, as a faith community, is relegated by the culture's frame of understanding to the private world of personal values, beliefs, and opinions. By and large, the church has willingly (if sometimes unknowingly) accommodated itself to that relegation and become a privatized, voluntary association for perpetuating its set of faith opinions. But for a church that believes that the gospel it embraces was God-given and intended as news for the whole world, for its public as well as its private life, there is a deep dilemma. We run the gauntlet between a failed Christendom and a false privatization, in pursuit of new ways of running it.

2. Lesslie Newbigin, *The Other Side of 1984: Questions for the Churches* (Geneva: World Council of Churches, 1983); *Foolishness to the Greeks: The Gospel and Western Culture* (Grand Rapids: Eerdmans, 1986); *The Gospel in a Pluralist Society* (Grand Rapids: Eerdmans, 1989).

We run the gauntlet in another way as well. When we recognize that what we are engaging is a cross-cultural missionary situation made more complicated by the fact that the culture in view is our own, we are thrown into serious difficulty. How can we critique our culture, and seek the gospel's critique of it, while our way of judging the culture and our way of reading the Bible are themselves shaped by our own culture? We are forced to develop approaches that navigate between the Scylla of culture bashing on the one side and the Charybdis of absorption into the culture on the other, attempting to avoid both dashing ourselves on the rocks and getting swallowed into the sea.

As much as Newbigin provides many helpful insights for taking up his challenge and running the gauntlet, probably his most important contribution is to have stimulated and framed the agenda. But it is important to recognize the ground from which that framing arises within the broader sweep of his missiological orientation. That will provide help along several lines: for interpreting his essential thesis, for recognizing its missiological character, and for identifying some of the contours for our engagement of the agenda within our own North American context.

Missiological Orientations

A Missiology of Culture

Foolishness to the Greeks is a book in two parts: the first ten pages, and then the remainder of the book. Those reading Newbigin who quickly judge that he holds a "Christ-against-culture" position and engages only in culture bashing have failed to recognize these two parts. The first contains in very distilled form a summary of his orientation toward the culturalness of human life, an orientation that has become standard for missiological reflections regarding places outside the West.[3] While his summary is remark-

---

3. H. Richard Niebuhr's classic text *Christ and Culture* (New York: Harper & Row, 1951) is not really an exception to that non-Western focus. His treatment has more to do with Christian attitudes and postures along the way in the journey of Western civilization and hardly raises the issues that arise with a contemporary anthropological understanding of "culture." The plurality of cultures in the world does not bear on his treatment. Increasingly, the categories of his paradigm fail to account for the complexities involved in Christian relationships to cultures and for the evolving configurations of Western culture. For these and many other reasons, the need for a new paradigm is one of the most pressing challenges we face.

ably unsophisticated in terms of cultural anthropology, it bears with great force the major insights of the global missionary experience and suggests that now we must do business the same way within our Western cultures. Perhaps more than anyone, Newbigin has grappled theologically with the issues of gospel and culture, not just from practical or strategic standpoints. Essential for understanding his proposal is an appreciation of the theology of cultural plurality that implicitly permeates these and others of his writings.[4]

At the heart of Newbigin's theology of cultural plurality lies his sense of a "three-cornered relationship" between the gospel, a particular culture, and the church.[5] Of special importance are the dynamics that emerge around each of the three axes formed: the conversion encounter axis, the reciprocal relationship axis, and the missionary dialogue axis (see fig. 1 on p. 14).

Along the first axis, the gospel and its communication present to every culture a "challenging relevance." It is relevant insofar as it is embodied in the terms by which people of the culture have learned to understand their world. It is challenging in that, in every culture, Jesus is introduced as one who bursts open the culture's models with the power of a wholly new fact.[6] Embodiment without challenge would lead to syncretism; challenge without embodiment would be irrelevant. This encounter between the gospel and a culture is a conversion encounter in that it precipitates a fundamental paradigm shift that brings about a new ultimate commitment at the center. It entails, in that sense, a "radical discontinuity," a break into new directions, for the one embracing the gospel. Never is this a total discontinuity, because the gospel and a person's response to it of necessity remain embodied in a particular culture's way of seeing, feeling, and acting.

The second axis, the reciprocal relationship between gospel and church, is the fruit of conversion. A community is established for whom

4. I explored this feature of Newbigin's missiology in "The Missionary Significance of the Biblical Doctrine of Election as a Foundation for a Theology of Cultural Plurality in the Missiology of J. E. Lesslie Newbigin" (PhD diss., Princeton Theological Seminary, 1987), later published by Eerdmans as *Bearing the Witness of the Spirit: Lesslie Newbigin's Theology of Cultural Plurality* (1998). Understanding the biblical doctrine of election as the inherent logic of mission (see Newbigin, *Foolishness to the Greeks*, pp. 53, 98-99, 127; *The Gospel in a Pluralist Society*, pp. 80ff.), Newbigin develops a theology of cultural plurality that provides theological grounding for discussions of cross-cultural mission, ecumenical relationship, and interfaith dialogue.

5. Lesslie Newbigin, *The Open Secret: Sketches for a Missionary Theology* (Grand Rapids: Eerdmans, 1978), pp. 165-72.

6. Lesslie Newbigin, "Christ and the Cultures," *Scottish Journal of Theology* 31, no. 1 (1978): 11-12.

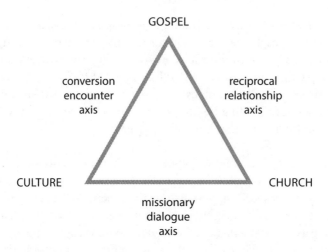

GOSPEL: "challenging relevance" in the culture
               "hermeneutical circle" with the church

CULTURE: radical discontinuity regarding the gospel
               radical independence regarding the church

CHURCH: adherence to the given tradition
               dialogue with the varied cultures

FIGURE 1. A Triangular Model of Gospel-Culture Relationships

"the Bible is the determinative clue to the character and activity of the one whose purpose is the final meaning of history."[7] But this community that is a "people of the book" is also the community that bears the Bible as its own testimony. The community's tradition shapes its reading of its book, while its reading and rereading of the book further shape its self-understanding. The church's commitment to the Bible's authority, embodied in an active discipleship, enables the hermeneutical circle between Bible and church itself to become the hermeneutic of the gospel among the cultures of the world.

The third axis is that between the missionary church and a local culture, regardless of how similar the two are culturally. The church's style of life becomes a missionary dialogue, which implies a multiplex church in full ecumenical dialogue among its own members in the variety of human cultures. Furthermore, it suggests that witness is always given with the rec-

7. Newbigin, *Foolishness to the Greeks,* p. 62.

ognition that, when heard and embraced, it is not the form of embodiment already achieved in the missionary church that will dictate the way conversion and discipleship will emerge in the new culture. Newbigin calls for a sense of the radical independence of the new convert (and newly converted church) vis-à-vis the missionary church through which the message has come. That complements the radical discontinuity of conversion itself, vis-à-vis one's own culture, and thus affirms the proper enculturedness of the forms that that conversion will take. Again, this radical independence cannot remain a total one, in that the new church takes its place alongside the other churches of the world in the necessary ecumenical conversation between the various inculturations of discipleship.

It is important to grasp these features of Newbigin's missionary approach that are briefly stated here. The authority of the Bible, its affirmation and critique of every culture, and the church's attitude toward both of these elements are essential for a serious missiological encountering of the Western culture that is for us in North American churches both our assumed reality and our missionary assignment. Newbigin's model helps us become more discriminating in our concern to avoid both syncretism and irrelevance, more focused upon inhabiting the biblical vision as part of a multicultural Christian community, and more open to the ongoing dialogue with our own culture, which is as much an inner dialogue as an outer one.

A Theology of Conversion

The second feature of Newbigin's missiological orientation that governs his approach to Western culture is his way of understanding conversion. He sees it as threefold. Conversion means "being turned round in order to recognize and participate in the dawning reality of God's reign. But this inward turning immediately and intrinsically involves both a pattern of conduct and a visible companionship. It involves membership in a community and a decision to act in certain ways."[8] For Newbigin, conversion has mental, ethical, and communal dimensions.

It is not accidental that the outline of *Foolishness to the Greeks* reflects this pattern.[9] After establishing his central thesis in the earlier chapters and showing how the missionary encounter he describes is borne by a commu-

---

8. Lesslie Newbigin, *The Finality of Christ* (Richmond, VA: John Knox Press, 1969), p. 96.
9. Page numbers in the text are from *Foolishness to the Greeks*.

nity that inhabits a different plausibility structure than that shared by the surrounding society, Newbigin takes up in turn these three dimensions of conversion. In chapter 4, entitled "Dialogue with Science," he demonstrates the "wider rationality" that can be claimed for Christian faith, which, unlike the predominant modern scientific worldview, does not exclude the category of purpose in regard to knowing (90). Chapter 5, "Dialogue with Politics," follows with the ethical dimension of conversion. There Newbigin portrays the calling of the church to be "resident aliens," embodying in its life "a witness to the kingship of Christ over all life — its political and economic no less than its personal and domestic morals" (102-3). In the final chapter, he gives a preliminary description of the resultant call to the church to recover "its proper distinction from, and its proper responsibility for, this secular culture that we have shared so comfortably and so long" (135). He asks the church to consider the forms of its life appropriate to a community governed by the vision of the coming reign of God (127-29, 134-37). In other words, the second half of this book is given over to an account of the shape of the radical paradigm shift to which the gospel calls the church in the midst of contemporary Western culture, a shift that leads to a new vision of how things are and, not all at once but gradually, to the development of a new plausibility structure in which the most real of all realities is the living God, whose character is rendered for us in the pages of Scripture (64).

This framework is important to recognize when one is tempted to see in Newbigin's proposals an accommodationism either to a residual Christendom model or to a ghettoized sectarianism.[10] He is attempting to avoid both and, as with all of us, runs the risk of falling prey to either. But whether or not his own specific visions for renewal and recovery achieve the goal, his pursuit is indeed governed by a fundamental conviction that whatever form the church's witness takes, it must represent a genuine and essential conversion of mind, behavior, and communal commitment.

A Postmodern Apologetic

It is perhaps Newbigin's richest contribution to Western Christian persons plagued by the nagging failure of nerve in regard to overt and explicit wit-

10. M. M. Thomas has taken the former position ("Mission and Modern Culture," *Ecumenical Review* 36, no. 3 [1984]: 316-22), Christopher B. Kaiser the latter ("The Foolishness of the 'Greeks,'" *Perspectives* 2, no. 4 [1987]: 7-9).

ness to a faith in Jesus Christ that he has supplied what I believe can be properly called a postmodern apologetic.[11] In a way that gives deep and empathetic response to the culture's intimidation that repels us into silence in all but our most formal opportunities to speak the gospel, Newbigin draws upon Michael Polanyi's sense of the ways of knowing in order to affirm the legitimate "rationality" of believing the gospel to be true, and true for all.[12] In so doing, he addresses not only the failure of nerve but its twin, the internal crisis of faith that it finally entails.

The most comprehensive development of this apologetic appears in *The Gospel in a Pluralist Society*. There, in the first five chapters, Newbigin seeks to provide a way of believing and knowing that shows how both scientists attempting to know physical objects and persons attempting to know God engage in the knowing in distinct but comparable ways. The supposed objective factuality of scientific knowing is broadly assumed in our culture to lie in contrast to religious conviction. But as Polanyi has observed, all knowing — scientific no less than religious — is subjective in that it is an act of personal commitment. Along with a focal dimension, it includes a tacit dimension of frames of reference and tools for knowing (including language) that are relied upon, at least for the moment, as investigation proceeds. Even doubt, as a knowing tool, rests upon beliefs held without doubting. In addition, all reasoning depends upon and is embodied within some rational tradition maintained within a particular community. In these ways, scientific knowing is not fundamentally different from religious knowing.

Religious knowing, which is likewise subjective, nevertheless bears features similar to those our culture has more readily assigned to scientific knowing. Personal knowing has an objective referent, and it is offered with universal intent. What is claimed to be known by "scientist" or "believer" is offered not as private opinion but as public fact and begs to be published and shared so that it can be questioned and checked in the public forum. In science as in religion, innovation is not so much by reason of new facts as by paradigm shift, and such shifts result from acts of imagination or intuition.

---

11. By introducing the term "postmodern" in reference to Newbigin's apologetic approach, I do not intend to make any particular claim regarding whether postmodernism is a newly emerging cultural paradigm, merely another extension and expression of modernity, or something more like the sense of a coming fin de siècle similar to that which expressed itself at the end of the nineteenth century (see Stjepan G. Mestrovic, *The Coming Fin de Siècle* [London: Routledge, 1991]).

12. See Michael Polanyi, *Personal Knowledge: Towards a Post-Critical Philosophy* (Chicago: University of Chicago Press, 1958).

It is the imagined "clue" that gives rise to advances in knowing. In the case of Christian faith, the gospel, the sense "that in the ministry, death, and resurrection of Jesus God has acted decisively to reveal and effect his purpose of redemption for the whole world,"[13] provides the clue to the meaning and purpose of the world's life.

Seen in the light of these observations about "personal knowing," religious knowing is no less credible than scientific knowing when both are rightly understood. In obvious ways, the apologetic Newbigin offers gives encouragement to move beyond intimidation, secure in the sense that the alternate "rational tradition" borne by the Christian community can be understood to be a credible "wider rationality" than that offered by the reigning plausibility structure of the culture. A sense of the ways we know gives rise to new ways of believing and witnessing.

The Missionary Congregation

A recurrent and forceful theme in Newbigin's missiology has been his challenge to the church to embody its true missionary character. Invariably, he focuses that challenge upon the fabric of the local congregation, emphasizing the necessity for visible unity among "all in each place" who believe the gospel and the implications of the catholicity of such truly united local bodies. Indeed, he has played a critical role in the definitions of unity and catholicity within World Council of Churches deliberations. Unity and catholicity are always crucial for Newbigin owing to their connection to the church's missionary character. A local church bears in itself all the marks of the catholic church and fully represents its fellowship to neighbors close at hand. That local church's unity is evidence that God has in fact sent Jesus into the world to be its savior. In that and a myriad of ways, the local congregation is the essential "hermeneutic of the gospel," the lens through which it may become known and by which it can rightly be interpreted.

The glaring absence of missionary character in the churches of the West has most alarmed Newbigin and has spurred his engagement of "the missionary encounter of the gospel with Western culture." That encounter, after all, is one that belongs to the heart and birthright of the church. So when he wrote *The Other Side of 1984*, it was in order to raise, as its subtitle states, "Questions for the Churches." *Foolishness to the Greeks* con-

13. Newbigin, *The Gospel in a Pluralist Society*, p. 5.

cludes with "Call to the Churches," focused on the question "What must we be?"[14] The concluding chapters of *The Gospel in a Pluralist Society* attempt to sketch the congregation's hermeneutical importance and the form of ministerial leadership required for such a missionary recovery. There, in a telling observation, he touches the raw nerve most illuminating of the central missiological problem for the Western churches: the need for recovering a practical missionary ecclesiology, a self-understanding of and by the churches that envisions our missionary character and guides us in faithful living. Newbigin observes:

> We have lived for so many centuries in the "Christendom" situation that ministerial training is almost entirely conceived in terms of the pastoral care of existing congregations. In a situation of declining numbers, the policy has been to abandon areas (such as inner cities) where active Christians are few and to concentrate ministerial resources by merging congregations and deploying ministers in the places where there are enough Christians to support them. Needless to say, this simply accelerates the decline. It is the opposite of a missionary strategy, which would proceed in the opposite direction — deploying ministers in the areas where the Christian presence is weakest. The large-scale abandonment of the inner cities by the "mainline" churches is the most obvious evidence of the policy that has been pursued.[15]

The implications for a domestic missiology for North America are important. There is a crisis touching the character of evangelism in a pluralist, secularist setting. But that crisis is first one of the identity of the church itself that renders its witness in such a setting. There is a crisis regarding the nature of the church's responsibility in and for the public order of the larger society. But that responsibility cries out for a new, post-Christendom definition of the church itself. The priority of questions surrounding the re-imaging of the church corresponds to Newbigin's long-standing convictions about the essential ecclesiological rootedness of the church's engagement in mission:

> The basic reality is the creation of a new being through the presence of the Holy Spirit. This new being is the common life (koinonia) in the

14. Newbigin, *Foolishness to the Greeks,* pp. 124ff.
15. Newbigin, *The Gospel in a Pluralist Society,* pp. 235-36.

Church. It is out of this new creation that both service and evangelism spring, and from it they receive their value. . . . These different acts have their relation to one another not in any logical scheme, but in the fact that they spring out of the one new reality.[16]

A North American Missiological Agenda

Most simply and directly put, it is the church's mission to represent the reign of God. It is the characteristic language of Newbigin to speak of the church as the "sign, instrument, and foretaste" of that reign,[17] language that has come to be shared broadly in ecumenical and Roman Catholic ecclesiology. It emphasizes that the church dare not equate itself with God's reign, which it only serves, but also it must avoid divorcing itself from that reign. As Newbigin has put it:

The . . . danger to be avoided is the separation of the Kingdom from the church. It is clear that they cannot and must not be confused, certainly not identified. But they must also not be separated. From the beginning the announcement of the Kingdom led to a summons to follow and so to the formation of a community. It is the community that has begun to taste (even only in foretaste) the reality of the Kingdom which can alone provide the hermeneutic of the message.[18]

In its mission under the reign of God, the church represents it as its community (koinonia), its servant (diakonia), and its messenger (kerygma). In its very life, as well as in its deeds and words, the church provides the locus and occasion for the Holy Spirit's manifestation of God's reign.[19] This basic understanding of what is properly the church's mission anywhere and anytime becomes suggestive regarding the mission of the moment for the churches in North America. The agenda before us gathers around three questions cast in light of the new circumstances: Christendom is gone, the church has been relegated to the private realm, and God is viewed by our contemporaries as neither necessary nor effective.

16. Lesslie Newbigin, *One Body, One Gospel, One World: The Christian Mission Today* (London: International Missionary Council, 1958), p. 20.
17. Newbigin, *The Open Secret*, p. 163; cf. *Foolishness to the Greeks*, p. 117.
18. Lesslie Newbigin, *Sign of the Kingdom* (Grand Rapids: Eerdmans, 1980), p. 19.
19. Newbigin, *Sign of the Kingdom*, p. 41.

With utmost seriousness, the churches of North America are faced with three matters of immediacy that are crucial for recovering our missionary character.

How Must We Grasp Our Identity?

In the latter half of the twentieth century the North American churches have experienced a great sea change in their social location and function. No sooner had the mid-century Protestant-Catholic-Jew consensus provided a place for the more formal elements of what Robert Bellah described as America's civil religion (e.g., inserting the phrase "under God" in the Pledge of Allegiance and adding "In God we trust" to our coinage) than we found ourselves experiencing a "restructuring of American religion." Robert Wuthnow documents the factors that have contributed first to a cleavage between two competing versions of civil religion and then to its collapse altogether.[20] As a result of these and other trends, we have come to a place in which the fundamental "legitimating myths" underlying the American social order have shifted. In place of "inalienable rights" with which we have been "endowed" by our Creator, the first principles have now come to be (1) freedom; (2) material success, as confirmation of the rightness of the freedom myth; and (3) technology, as the infrastructure supporting the other two. What was once "freedom in the interests of religious faith" has become "faith under the protective cover of freedom." Freedom has become the "guiding principle that needs no further justification or definition." Religion is seen merely as a story that illustrates the value of freedom.[21]

Such a shift means a change in social location for the churches. As Kennon Callahan has put it in more popular fashion, "The day of the churched culture is over."[22] The day has gone when the church was generally valued by the society as important to the social and moral order and when, for that reason, people tended to seek out a church for themselves. We sail today in a different kind of sea.

If our caretaker days are over and the church is no longer looked to for legitimation or moral underpinning, we have scarcely begun to live as

---

20. Robert Wuthnow, *The Restructuring of American Religion: Society and Faith since World War II* (Princeton: Princeton University Press, 1988), chap. 10.

21. Wuthnow, *The Restructuring of American Religion,* chap. 11.

22. Kennon L. Callahan, *Effective Church Leadership* (San Francisco: Harper & Row, 1990), p. 13.

though that were true, which explains why we experience these changes as a crisis. The Christendom experiment has run its course and is over, but our images and instincts are still formed by its memory. We play out the church's routine as though the concerns of the church and the quests of the culture go hand-in-glove. We are never quite sure which is the hand and which the glove, but we are certain they form common cause. The rude awakening breaking in on us is that whatever such connection there may have been in the past, it is vanishing.

We are caught between a Constantinian Christendom that has ended and to which we cannot return and the culture's relegation of the church to the private realm, which is untenable if we have understood rightly that the gospel is news that has relevance to the public life of the whole world.[23] Repeatedly, the image of exile has best seemed to capture who we have become and how we might live in hope in the place of our planting.[24] Perhaps the image is especially pertinent because in its dislocation an exile community feels most keenly the loss — or simply the absence — of a clear sense of its identity or a focused center for its life. To know itself as exile is the beginning of recovery.

Israel's experience of exile in Babylon elicits a rich tapestry of identity for the church in a new exile. Exiles hold the ultimate power to name themselves (Dan. 1; cf. John 1:12). Or, more accurately, they have the freedom to use the names given them by the empire while boldly retaining names that assert its limits! They are possessed of promises that this is not the way things will end, while carrying instructions to seek the welfare of the city in the meantime (Jer. 29:1-14). They are full of danger for the empire, driven by dangerous memories and promises, expressing themselves with dangerous songs and criticism, eating dangerous bread, and making dangerous departures.[25] They are at once both a "chosen out" people of distinct character and a "scattered abroad" (diaspora) people of common similarity (1 Pet. 1:1-2).

---

23. Newbigin, *Foolishness to the Greeks*, pp. 101-2.

24. The most complete depiction of an exilic model comes from Stanley Hauerwas and William H. Willimon, *Resident Aliens: Life in the Christian Colony* (Nashville: Abingdon Press, 1989). Others who move in this direction include Ephraim Radner, in his article "From 'Liberation' to 'Exile': A New Image for Church Mission," *Christian Century*, 18 October 1989, pp. 931-34; Walter Brueggemann, in *Disciplines of Readiness* (Louisville: Theology and Worship Unit, Presbyterian Church [U.S.A.], 1988); and Jeremiah Wright, in an unpublished address given in 1988 at the presidential inauguration at Tougaloo College, Jackson, Mississippi.

25. Brueggemann, *Disciplines of Readiness*; cf. Isa. 40–55.

Stanley Hauerwas and William Willimon propose a "confessing church" model as a "radical alternative" to the "activist" (Constantinian) or "conversionist" (privatized) models that are current. What they envision is the church as "an alternative *polis,* a countercultural social structure called church." Such a church has as its overriding political task "to be the community of the cross." They wish to see a church "that again asserts that God, not nations, rules the world, that the boundaries of God's kingdom transcend those of Caesar, and that the main political task of the church is the formation of people who see clearly the cost of discipleship and are willing to pay the price." They invite us to see ourselves with exilic eyes as "resident aliens, an adventurous colony in a society of unbelief."[26]

The inevitable charge that these proposals constitute a new sectarianism warns of a danger that a sharper sense of being an alternative community will make the church aloof from the culture's need for its healing presence. But being "of" the world (culture) has never been a better guarantee that the church is "in" the world.[27] In fact, only by adopting alternative principles can the church free itself from the social segregation it experiences at the hand of the culture's principles. Already in the early 1970s, George Lindbeck predicted what he termed "the sectarian future of the church." He noted that "to the degree generalized social support disappears, it becomes necessary for Christians or members of any other deviant minority to gather together in small, cohesive, mutually supportive groups. They must become, sociologically speaking, sectarian." This is different from an ecclesiastical or theological sectarianism that splinters into competing groups. The early church, a "strongly deviant minority, unsupported by cultural convention and prestige," remained "catholic" and "ecumenical" for all its diversity.[28] It was the merging of that sociological sectarianism with the divisive and schismatic theological variety that has plagued the church subsequently. A recovery of the sociological form without its attachment to the ecclesiastical form is Lindbeck's proposal for a responsible sectarianism for our age.

The practical agenda that emerges in light of our present circumstances includes four basic tasks for congregations and their leaders. Two relate to the healing of the church's identity and its intimidation: (1) forming an alternate, communal "world"; and (2) casting a "wider rationality."

26. Hauerwas and Willimon, *Resident Aliens,* pp. 44-49.

27. See Donald C. Posterski, *Reinventing Evangelism: New Strategies for Presenting Christ in Today's World* (Downers Grove, IL: InterVarsity Press, 1989), p. 28.

28. George A. Lindbeck, "The Sectarian Future of the Church," in *The God Experience,* ed. Joseph P. Whelan, SJ (New York: Newman Press, 1971), pp. 227, 230.

The other two concern the church's inner and outer dialogue with the culture: (3) healing our fragmentary "worlds" (work, home, leisure, commerce, education, politics, church, etc.); and (4) igniting a subversive witness.[29]

How Must We Seek the "Common Good"?

An exilic image helps, rather than hurts, the church's inclination toward seeking the common good, if properly understood. But if Jeremiah's letter to the exiles in Babylon provides any guidance at all in that regard, it is to be found in the absence of Constantinian language (Jer. 29:1-14). The exiles were to seek the welfare of the city, but not from any impulse that they must somehow seize control of its policies and dictate its ideology. Nor was their welfare-seeking to be done in order to justify themselves as pragmatically useful in the eyes of the ruling ethos, as the church has been pressed to do in modern American society. The impetus to seek the city's welfare was not even to be borne along by expectations of success in refashioning the shape of Babylon, but only by the recognition that their service announced greater realities than those upon which the Babylonian society was based (see Dan. 3:16-18).

If the Christendom image of our fit in the social scheme of things has played out and our prior sense of social responsibility was largely attached to it (in the espousal of both liberal and conservative agendas), what new sense must we gain of our God-given call to seek the common good? In a religiously and ideologically plural setting, what is the place of Christian visions for what makes the common order "good"? How must they be sought or offered amid the alternate visions? If we seek the good not from a hope of success, then from what hope can we find motivation for representing the justice, peace, and joy of the reign of God? A new cast to the very way we ask the questions is called for.

While the carving of new paths for our thinking and action will not be easy and cannot be quickly achieved, at least several contours would appear to be important features for the way ahead. First, we must be self-conscious that *we offer our action for the common good within a pluralist setting and according to pluralist rules.* While the church seeks and finds its own identity beyond the definitions given by the culture, we cannot expect our participa-

---

29. George R. Hunsberger, "The Changing Face of Ministry: Christian Leadership for the Twenty-First Century," *Reformed Review* 44, no. 3 (Spring 1991): 224-45.

tion in the social struggles to follow our rules. In this respect we will need to learn from the churches of the world that live out responsibility for the common good from their positions as minorities. The dynamics of mission in weakness and persistence at the margins will need to characterize our work.

Second, *our pursuit of the common good must be marked by a more rigorous holism.* The polarization between Christian action for social justice and Christian action for personal morality is problematic because both too easily represent an accommodation to the culture's individualist rights and interests. If the church only mimics the culture's loosening grip on the question about that which serves the *common* good and reflects the same tendency toward single-issue politics and constituency satisfaction, there will be little contribution that will distinguish the character of the coming reign of God the church represents.

Third, *our action for the common good requires more complete communal integrity within the church.* Whatever we espouse for the good of the society must be demonstrated by a living community that believes the vision enough to form its life around it. Ephraim Radner describes the shift implied as a movement from our tendency to think in terms of totalistic, theocratic transformation (a liberationist model) toward the recovery of a sense that it is "the growth and expansion of religious communities, separate but within the larger society, that will engender vehicles for noncoercive deliverance."[30] The church that pronounces concern for the homeless on the White House lawn, based on a set of values at odds with the culture, will welcome the homeless themselves into the shelter of their homes and houses of worship. For that integrity, Radner suggests, the image of exile serves better than one of liberation. In that image, the church becomes "a vessel of deliverance" rather than its agent.

Fourth, *our care for the common good must grow from a care-filled eschatology.* To say it that way is to distinguish such an eschatology from an overly "careful" (in the sense of reticent) eschatology that holds back from risk taking and vulnerability. It also distinguishes it from a "careless" (in the sense of reckless) eschatology that blusters on triumphalistically. We must learn a pursuit of the common good that sets aside both our hand-wringing and our utopianisms, both our hand-washing self-justifications and our demanding impositions. It is the reign *of God,* after all, that is coming, our assurance of which creates confident and humble action.

---

30. Radner, "From 'Liberation' to 'Exile,'" p. 933.

How Must We Tell the Gospel?

The third critical issue facing churches wishing to recover their missionary character is evangelism. From one perspective, the issue concerns telling the gospel in terms appropriate to an audience of people who live with post-Christian, secular convictions. As George Hunter has pointed out, the genius of such diverse people as Samuel Shoemaker, Robert Schuller, and Bill Hybels lies in the seriousness with which they saw and pursued the matter of communicating with secular people.[31] Such a nuancing of our gospel-telling, lacking for the most part in the dominant programs of evangelism, is a long overdue development.[32]

But something more crucial is needed. The very way in which we conceive evangelism needs an overhaul. We cannot expect that in our new circumstances its shape as a Christian practice will not be remade. At least four features are implicated in that renewal.

1. We have already hinted that it is important to the vitality of today's churches to show that the Christian faith provides a "wider rationality" than that of a culture for which the reigning paradigm explains things in terms of cause and effect without any recourse to questions of purpose. The silenced witness of the church grows out of the intense intimidation that the culture breeds. Here is where Newbigin's postmodern apologetics helps. Unless North American Christians are helped to find confidence in *ways of knowing* that are demonstrably rational but liberated from false cultural shackles, there is hardly a way to expect witness to emerge. Our guilt-ridden motivational strategies and church growth technologies will never provide adequate substitutes.

2. A tandem requirement is that evangelism be grounded in a *credible demonstration* that life lived by the pattern of commitment to Jesus is imaginable, possible, and relevant in the modern and postmodern age. This requires more than what we meant previously when we called for verbal witness to rest on consistent Christian living. That tended to mean living exemplary, moral lives as upstanding citizens. The requirements of moral faithfulness are no less now; more important, though, the current need is for a demonstration that a faith in the gospel of God can be the genuine

31. George G. Hunter III, "Communicating Christianity to Secular People" (church growth lectures, Fuller Theological Seminary, 1989).

32. See George G. Hunter III, *How to Reach Secular People* (Nashville: Abingdon Press, 1992), which explores important features of this issue.

organizing center integrating the fragmented pieces of modern living. Only when that is seen lived out by someone who believes that way will the message about the reign of God have credibility. "The gospel will be perceived as a feasible alternative when those who do not know God have some positive, personal experiences with people who do."[33]

3. A reshaped evangelism will include a new *willingness to influence*. It is, perhaps, Donald Posterski's most important contribution to the "reinventing" of evangelism that he seizes the horns of the pluralism dilemma and offers a way to witness by going into and through the culture's pluralist assumptions rather than an evangelistic stance formed out of resistance and opposition to those dynamics. He encourages a style that moves alongside "the principles that govern a pluralistist society: acceptance of diversity . . . , appreciation of options . . . , and interaction with alternatives." He judges that the tolerance factor in pluralism is an open opportunity for evangelism, not a barrier that stymies it. "When people sense they are accepted and appreciated for who they are, they are ready to interact without being defensive."[34] An evangelistic style, therefore, that begins with acceptance and appreciation will have gained the opportunity and freedom to influence.

4. All of this implies a deepening *humility of witness*. New images commend themselves. Newbigin suggests the image of a witness giving testimony "in a trial where it is contested" and where the verdict "will only be given at the end." It is the function of such a witness "not to develop conclusions out of already known data, but simply to point to, report, affirm that which cannot come into the argument at all except simply as a new datum, a reality which is attested by a witness."[35] David Lowes Watson has suggested a shift from a sales model to a journalist model, keying on the recognition that evangelism is a global announcement that the reign of God is at hand.[36] Another model that commends itself in an age requiring that evangelists become meaning-makers is that of docent, in the sense of its use in museums and the Atlanta Zoo.[37] At the latter, docents are volunteers trained to mix among the crowds and be available to explain the various animal behaviors and habitats, providing interpretations of the worlds represented in

33. Posterski, *Reinventing Evangelism*, p. 32.

34. Posterski, *Reinventing Evangelism*, pp. 168, 169.

35. Newbigin, *Foolishness to the Greeks*, p. 64; Leslie Newbigin, *The Light Has Come: An Exposition of the Fourth Gospel* (Grand Rapids: Eerdmans, 1982), p. 14.

36. David Lowes Watson, "The Church as Journalist: Evangelism in the Context of the Local Church in the United States," *International Review of Mission* 72 (January 1983): 57-74.

37. See Posterski, *Reinventing Evangelism*, pp. 31-48.

the exhibits. Evangelism implies casting the "wider rationality" of a world seen as the location of the saving purposes of God.

Paying Attention

Such an agenda will require us to be more attentive in several areas. If our practical missiology points us toward developing patterns of life, deed, and word, the wider missiological task includes the attention we give in three other directions.

First, we must *pay attention to the culture.* For us to assume we know it has cost too much. It has led too easily to accommodation. Only an insightful analysis of the cultural and social systems shaping, and being shaped by, life in North America can enable us to keep our missiology contextual. Current studies in these areas are plentiful. The special need is for missiologically sensitive readings of America's cultural history, of the new sociological histories of the role and fate of the churches, and of the depictions of current cultural trends and future scenarios.

Second, we must *pay attention to the gospel.* A theological agenda here must correspond to the phenomenological one. The central question of theology — What is the gospel? — must be asked in greater culturally particular ways. And the more particular the question, the greater will be our sense that the answer will emerge in unexpected ways. It will come more out of Christian communities that increasingly learn the habit of "indwelling" the gospel story so deeply that it shapes their life of common discipleship.[38] The meaning of work and vocation, the integrating of our pluralistic experience, and a declericalized relocation of theology to the province of the laity are all implicated as elements of a missiologically sensitive theological agenda.

Third, we must *pay attention to each other.* It will require of us a new range of "ecumenical" partnership if we are to hear the gospel as it takes form in the variety of cultures, subcultures, denominational cultures, and ethnic cultures of North America. There is no substitute for that breadth of listening if the forms of our common mission are to be seriously directed toward the dominant undercurrents of the culture as a whole. At this point, the agenda takes on global dimensions because the growing pervasiveness of Western culture, carrying with it its pattern of resistance to the gospel,

38. See Newbigin, *The Gospel in a Pluralist Society,* p. 232.

has made the agenda Newbigin has fostered a world-encircling one. Our openness to help from the world church and its own missionary encounter with our culture can no longer be avoided. We are one church in our common mission to represent the reign of God in a modern, secular, pluralist world.

A Vendor-Shaped Church

1994

The Winter 1993-94 issue of *Reformed Review* contains a collection of articles whose aim it is to "size up" the Reformed Church in America (RCA), with a look at the fortunes of the whole as well as the experience of several of its parts. The articles include a look at the past and hints of dreams for the future. They pay attention to factors both within and without the church.

But there is an essential problematic that remains to be uncovered. It becomes evident when the myth-breaking study of Roger Nemeth and Donald Luidens takes a prescriptive turn. The advice that the RCA "needs to be more intentional in reaching out to groups that have not been well represented in the denomination if membership trends are to be reversed" comes on the heels of their dramatic news that during the last century RCA membership has essentially grown, and now declined, as a consequence of the rate of having babies.[1] How does a centuries-long habit in which "membership trends were principally dependent upon 'natural' growth" shift toward a new spurt of intentionality in recruitment? What historic character or quality would that shift hope to draw upon? What would it take to recast dramatically the corporate culture of the churches, and where does the hope lie that the churches could or would, with a flash of recognition, decide to make such dramatic changes? What would motivate the change?

The suggestion to "be more intentional" — that is, beef up our evan-

---

1. Roger J. Nemeth and Donald A. Luidens, "The Reformed Church in the Larger Picture: Facing Structural Realities," *Reformed Review* 47, no. 2 (Winter 1993-94): 94.

gelistic fortitude — too easily underwrites the now all-too-familiar habit of thinking that the signs of crisis in the church are really not so dire, that with a bit of tweaking and tuning a midcourse correction can turn the fortunes around, and that if we try harder, we can move out of the doldrums.

But the crisis *is* dire. Tuning the engine and trying harder will not change the growing malaise in the churches or their increasing experience of being finally and firmly "disestablished" from roles of importance we thought we had in the larger society. The fundamental crisis we are facing is the one Douglas John Hall calls a *crisis of thinking.*[2] In particular, it is a crisis of thinking about what the church is and how we fit into the scheme of things in the world. Or perhaps more accurately, the crisis is that we have *not* thought carefully, critically, or theologically about our assumptions regarding the church and have failed to notice how much they have been shaped by the character of modern American life.

Shape, Not Size

Our current *crisis of size* is only a symptom of deeper and broader changes in the form and place of religious life in North American society. The crisis of size should therefore be recognized as a signal that we are facing a more pressing crisis, a *crisis of shape.* The fact that we experience the current crisis primarily as one of size is itself one of the important clues to the crisis of shape: namely, we have come to regard the church as being in the religion business, and right now sales are down.

The crisis of shape about which I am speaking is by its nature a theological crisis, one of great magnitude and consequence. It is theological because it has to do with how we understand what was and is in God's mind regarding this social configuration called "church." But it is important to clarify that in calling attention to the theological nature of this crisis, I am not contradicting one of the most important points made by Nemeth and Luidens. They show that the factors involved in the decline of the denomination "are of long standing, and generally pre-date any of the ideological debates of 'left' and 'right' that are so audible and high-voltage." The changes, they say, "seem to be little impressed by this noisy polemic." They show that the winding down of the RCA's "market share" of American church adherents was well under way at the beginning of the century and that the shift

2. Douglas John Hall, *Thinking the Faith* (Minneapolis: Augsburg Press, 1989), p. 12.

of monies from denominational to local and congregational needs occurred well before the turbulent 1960s. Their point is well made that the normal scapegoats do not qualify when assessing the causes of decline. The intramural, ideological battles were not factors. Nor was the organizational restructuring or changes in denominational leadership. Nemeth and Luidens insist that "we must look to the social structural context within which the RCA and other denominations function in order to learn what happened to the membership trends."[3]

To find reasons for decline in the broader social context does not mean that there are not internal, theological ones. Luidens, in collaboration with several other scholars, demonstrates this point. In an article entitled "Mainline Churches: The Real Reason for Decline," Luidens and his companions report the findings of a study of the religious attitudes and practices of baby boomers who had been confirmed in mainline Protestant churches (in particular, the Presbyterian Church [U.S.A.]) during the 1960s. They found that "the single best predictor of church participation turned out to be *belief* — orthodox Christian belief, and especially the teaching that a person can be saved only through Jesus Christ." They concluded that mainline denominations "seem to be weak in the sense of being unable to generate and maintain high levels of commitment among a substantial portion of their adherents." This they attribute in part to the fact that denominational leaders did not, in response to the currents of modernity, "devise or promote compelling new versions of a distinctively Christian faith. They did not fashion or preach a vigorous apologetics." The advice is that "if the mainline churches want to regain their vitality, their first step must be to address theological issues head-on."[4]

Another study that has gained a lot of attention is the seven-volume series entitled *The Presbyterian Presence: The Twentieth-Century Experience.* In the concluding volume, the editors of the series (Milton J Coalter, John M. Mulder, and Louis B. Weeks) draw together the fruits of the massive study. There they write that "fragmentation of its life and witness . . . best explains the historical contours of twentieth-century American Presbyterianism." This interpretation has value, they say, because it suggests that "the problems of American mainstream Protestantism are not due simply to human mistakes or institutional missteps; rather, the difficulties are part of

---

3. Nemeth and Luidens, "Reformed Church," p. 85.

4. Benton Johnson, Dean R. Hoge, and Donald A. Luidens, "Mainline Churches: The Real Reason for Decline," *First Things* 31 (March 1993): 13-18.

the broad process of modernization that has shaped so much of twentieth-century American culture."[5]

Having summarized the most important findings of the study, Coalter, Mulder, and Weeks conclude with a chapter entitled "An Agenda for Reform." The agenda in the end is a theological one. They suggest five crucial "theological questions posed by these epochal changes." The fourth is especially pertinent to the theological issue I am raising about the shape of the church:

> Why, after all, is there a church — an ordered community of Christians? Why is faith a communal experience, rather than a private one? Swirling beneath the sociological trends in American society is not only the institutional crisis of American Presbyterianism and mainstream Protestantism but the haunting query of individuals about the need for and purpose of the church. . . . The church's community must have a forthright and compellingly persuasive vision of what the church is and should be for Christian witness.[6]

While we need to understand the sociological trends that influence our churches, our calling to witness faithfully to Jesus Christ requires that we also give keen attention to the theological issues implicated in our analysis of the trends.

I am suggesting that beneath the ebb and flow of contextual factors lies a substructure of commonly accepted notions about the church and its public role that has gone largely undetected. There is need for theological analysis that goes beyond discussions about the changing context or the effect of ecclesiastical debates and gets at this substructure.

The Church as a Vendor of Religious Services

What is the present shape of the church? The question must be asked honestly. Simple references to biblical phrases or creedal definitions may mask what is really operating in our day-to-day notions, which have much more

---

5. Milton J Coalter, John M. Mulder, and Louis B. Weeks, *The Re-Forming Tradition: Presbyterians and Mainstream Protestantism* (Louisville: Westminster/John Knox Press, 1992), p. 24.

6. Coalter, Mulder, and Weeks, *The Re-Forming Tradition*, pp. 283-84.

to do with our actions and choices. David Bosch addressed this issue in lectures on the eve of the publication of his major work *Transforming Mission*.[7] He noted that we Protestants have inherited a particular view of the church from the Reformers. Their emphases on the marks of the true church — the right preaching of the gospel, the right administration of the sacraments, and the exercise of church discipline — have bequeathed to us an understanding that the church is "a place where certain things happen." However, in this century this view has been changing. The fruits of the missionary movement and the emergence of a global church have led us to see that the church is essentially "a body of people sent on a mission."[8] This he identified as a crucial element in the "emerging ecumenical paradigm" of mission.

Bosch has surely put his finger on an important twentieth-century rediscovery of a biblical perspective. But is that the way that congregations conceive themselves and live? In North America, we live out of a very different model, even when we mouth formal statements like the one Bosch articulates. We are not very far from the notion that the church is "a place where certain things happen." Our common language betrays that. Church is something you "go to." We ask, "Where is your church?" The word may refer to a building, but even when it does not, it tends to refer to an institution as embodied by officers and staff or to a set of programs offered according to a certain schedule of days and times. When I was a child, we talked about "going to Sunday school and church," a statement in which the word "church" referred to the Sunday morning eleven o'clock worship service.

More specifically, though, our contemporary notion is a variation on the "place where" way of defining the church. In the North American setting, we have come to view the church as "a vendor of religious services and goods" (see fig. 1 on p. 35). To this notion we attach the language of production, marketing, sales, and consumption. A congregation becomes a retail outlet or franchise of the denominational brand. Staff at all levels become sales and service representatives. The denomination is the corporate headquarters in charge of everything from research and development to mass media imaging.

Most of us value the use of many businesslike techniques and procedures in the life of the church but would be aghast at the suggestion that we

7. David J. Bosch, *Transforming Mission: Paradigm Shifts in Theology of Mission* (Maryknoll, NY: Orbis, 1991).

8. David J. Bosch, in lectures given at Western Theological Seminary, Holland, Michigan, April 1991.

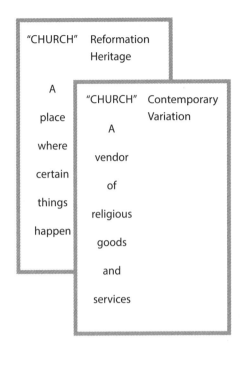

"CHURCH" Reformation Heritage

A place where certain things happen

"CHURCH" Contemporary Variation

A vendor of religious goods and services

"CHURCH" Missionary Vision

A body of people sent on a mission

FIGURE 1

fundamentally operate out of a model of the church as a business, a vendor of religious services. But consider the unconscious and unquestioned form of many of our carefully worded mission statements. It is amazing how many are cast something like this: "The mission of Anytown Community Church is to nurture its members in Christian faith and equip them for service and witness to Christ in the world." What follows tends to detail the educational, worship, witness, and justice commitments of the church. But notice how the text reads. The mission of this *church* is to nurture its *members*. In a statement like that, to what does the word "church" refer? It sits over against the members, for whom it has a mission to do certain things. Church here refers either to the official governing body that feels responsible to meet the needs of the members of the congregation or those outside it, or to the staff whom they charge with that responsibility. But the members are not conceived, in such a statement, as *being* the church and themselves *having* a mission on which they have been collectively sent.

Instead, they are the customers, the regular consumers for whom the religious services and goods produced by the "church" are intended. On such a model, evangelism devolves into membership recruitment, which may more accurately be called "capturing market share." This kind of "church" is in the business of religion, and its livelihood is dependent on having a sufficient number of satisfied, committed customers.

In their study, Nemeth and Luidens give hints along this same line. They report the findings of Roger Finke and Rodney Stark that "a major change in organizational thinking hit Protestant circles in the late 1800s." Following developments in industry and business, churches incorporated models of efficiency and rationalization, implementing consolidation and specialization with a view toward an "economy of scale." They conclude: "Finke and Stark argue that this rationalizing and consolidating movement led directly to the demise of a sense of religious community among members of mainline congregations."[9]

Nemeth and Luidens go on to show how postwar "professionalization of the church and the decline of traditional volunteerism" (which may not be so unconnected as they imply) affected congregational spending patterns. They report that dominant concerns in that era included such things as raising the standards of services, upgrading programs and facilities, widening the scope of programs offered, and using paid experts to run programs, all of which were part of the congregations' answer to "the call to a heightened competition for new members."[10]

The difficulty comes when we fail to see that these developments are all theological. Nemeth and Luidens imply they are not, an implication that is heightened by their (rightful) emphasis on the influence of the context on membership trends. But many trends, particularly external ones that shape the church's self-understanding, are very theological and must be examined as such.

For example, the structural revolution in the churches at the beginning of the century is important because it is part of a much longer development that has shaped the American church's notion of itself and has structured its life. The pervasiveness of this shaping is underscored by the approach used in the study of Finke and Stark to which Nemeth and Luidens refer. The study assumes an economic understanding of religious life and practice that has been characteristic of the American setting. Finke

9. Nemeth and Luidens, "The Reformed Church," p. 89.
10. Nemeth and Luidens, "The Reformed Church," p. 92.

and Stark defend the persistent use of "market" terminology by making the case "that where religious affiliation is a matter of choice, religious organizations must compete for members and that the 'invisible hand' of the marketplace is as unforgiving of ineffective religious firms as it is of their commercial counterparts." They use "economic concepts such as markets, firms, market penetration, and segmented markets to analyze the success and failure of religious bodies" and in the process evaluate clergy as sales representatives, religious doctrines as product, and evangelization techniques as marketing techniques.[11]

Finke and Stark do not defend this approach as a good theology of the church but regard it as the necessary historical and sociological tool for assessing its disestablishment, a situation that resulted in churches operating like business firms in a religious economy. They note that "religious economies are like commercial economies in that they consist of a market made up of a set of current and potential customers and a set of firms seeking to serve that market."[12] This form of analysis, they believe, best corresponds to the experience of the churches. But by making their case they show how much the churches of North America have come to live out of a long-standing notion that a church is a vendor of religious services and goods.

A Body of People Sent on a Mission

It is frankly hard to conceive of the reaction Christians of the New Testament era would have had to the notion of the church as a religious vendor. It is thoroughly foreign to the New Testament portrayals of the nature and style of the church's presence in the communities of that time. The New Testament never envisioned a church that was defined in so economic a way. Churches were not business firms. They were living, pulsing communities grasped by the news that the light and salvation of the world had come in Jesus Christ. As a consequence, their relations to the world were changed. They represented to the world the news that had seized them. They did not look for religious customers; they gave the gospel away to the spiritually hungry and thirsty.[13]

---

11. Roger Finke and Rodney Stark, *The Churching of America, 1776-1990: Winners and Losers in Our Religious Economy* (New Brunswick, NJ: Rutgers University Press, 1992), p. 17.

12. Finke and Stark, *The Churching of America*, p. 17.

13. It may be worth noting that much church growth literature appears to contradict this understanding of the New Testament. In this literature, the concern for size and growth

The prevalence of the vendor notion in our understandings today, and the disjuncture between that notion and anything the New Testament suggests, indicate that we are face to face here with the most basic of theological questions. The question is crucial, especially in a day when we struggle so hard as denominations and congregations to ascertain our identity. Our identity crisis must achieve this level of theological engagement if we are to find our way again.

How, then, do we shift from the structure of church life that revolves around the vendor notion to one that forms itself around the notion that we are "a body of people sent on a mission"? If we do not recognize such a shift to be a tall order, we have not grasped the seriousness of the difference. And if we think that we can easily extricate ourselves from one operating assumption and implement another, we do not comprehend how historically rooted the church always is and must be. But our historical rooting can never be an excuse for avoiding change. We are always subject to the gospel's call to make fundamental departures from assumptions about ourselves that the surrounding society holds. It is that call which we need to allow.

Nothing close to a full answer to our question can be given here. But several aspects of the necessary re-forming of the church may begin to indicate something of the path we must take.

The Church Localized

First, we need to localize our sense of the church. This is the burden of the recent organizational ferment in the Presbyterian Church (U.S.A.). The study edited by Coalter, Mulder, and Weeks traced the rise of the "corporate denomination" beginning at the end of the nineteenth century. "The denomination as a corporation is a bureaucratic, hierarchical organization de-

---

so characteristic of churches living out of a "religious economy" model is defended as theologically appropriate because the Great Commission leads us to expect growth as a dynamic of the church. But even when that growth criterion is redeemed, as it is in the hand of Charles Van Engen (who makes "yearning for growth," and not growth itself, the mark of the true church), what remains unexamined is the operative notion of "church" with which we are dealing and the way that has been so reshaped in our modern American experience that the biblical growth motifs become irrelevant to it. The biblical motifs are speaking in reference to a form of church other than a "vendor of religious services." See Charles E. Van Engen, *The Growth of the True Church* (Amsterdam: Rodopi, 1981).

pendent on managers and capable of delivering goods and services to congregations as well as mobilizing and coordinating support of national and
international mission causes." Some have suggested that this trend led ultimately to a two-church model: the national, corporate church and the local
church of the congregations. The widening gap between the two brought
about the unraveling of the corporate denomination, and the outcome is
not entirely evident. What is evident, however, is that "the congregation is
now the locus of power and mission in American Presbyterianism."[14] Recent restructuring in the PC(USA) intends to embed that understanding in
the denominational structures.

This shift in the locus of mission makes denominational systems ner-
vous. Frequently in Reformed and Presbyterian circles it leads to a knee-
jerk charge of "creeping congregationalism." In reality the shift is a reversal
of the "creeping denominationalism" of the last centuries and a reemergence of what I would prefer to call *congregationism.* "Congregationalism"
refers to the system of church government that maintains the autonomy of
the local congregation. In contrast, "congregationism" retains a sense of the
mutuality and accountability of congregations with each other but stresses
that the mission and identity of the church takes form most essentially in
the local congregation.[15]

This shift of locus provides a critique of the vendor model of the
church, which became especially prominent in the corporate denomination. Another line of critique shows how the corporate denomination was
designed around a "modern" style of business organization that is itself
experiencing change in a postmodern situation. Nancy Ammerman has
provided an analysis of the current struggles within the Southern Baptist
Convention that suggests that we are seeing the emergence of new forms
of denominational style. The contrast is between modern organizations (of
which the corporate denomination is an example) and postmodern ones.
What made sense as an economy of scale in the modern organization has
now become subject to a pluralized and fragmented marketplace (religious
or otherwise) in which one size does not fit all. Ammerman illustrates the
forces at work in this transition by giving a series of comparisons. In regard
to the activities of the organization, it means a shift from mass produc-

14. Coalter, Mulder, and Weeks, *The Re-Forming Tradition,* p. 101.
15. Discussions on the theme of the unity and catholicity of the church at the New
Delhi (1961) and Uppsala (1968) assemblies of the World Council of Churches give shape to
such an understanding.

tion to finding niches. In regard to technology, it is based on the shift from technological determinism to a range of technological choices. As regards organization, it entails a shift from highly specialized to highly generalized styles. Regarding relationships, it means a move from a large and centralized organization to a decentralized and flexible one.[16]

Two movements are going on here. On the one hand, the locus of the church's vitality and mission is being reassigned to the local congregation. On the other hand, there are revised patterns emerging in denominational structures. What must be observed is that these shifts, important as they are, do not get at the root of the problem. They do not question deeply enough the vendor notion of the church. The shift to a postmodern style may relieve the pressures building in the modern form of organization, but denominations may continue to function in a vendor manner. If the shift from a denominational locus of identity and mission to a congregational one in any way opens up a critique of the vendor model, then it simply begs the question at the congregational level. As Coalter, Mulder, and Weeks observe, "The impulse toward incorporation permeated congregations, as well as national structures."[17] So a shift from modern to postmodern organization would be as important for the congregation as it is for the denomination. But even more fundamental is the question whether a vendor model is theologically faithful or adequate. In addition to localizing the church, therefore, we must test the way local congregations structure their life and must look for the revolutions that are needed there.

Practical Shifts

A number of practical shifts will be necessary if we are to move from treating the church as a vendor of religious services to being a body of people sent on a mission.

A shift from program to embodiment. It makes a difference whether a church is oriented toward producing programs and services for potential consumers, or whether it is committed to cultivating habits of life that help us be faithful to the gospel together. The latter focuses attention on how we

16. Nancy T. Ammerman, "SBC Moderates and the Making of a Postmodern Denomination," *Christian Century,* 22-29 September 1993, pp. 896-99.

17. Milton J Coalter, John M. Mulder, and Louis B. Weeks, "Revolution and Survival," *Presbyterian Survey,* January/February 1992, p. 14.

embody the gospel and how we make it light, salt, seed, and aroma for the world around us. Our identity as a community of disciples must again be the center of our life together. Programs must be clearly subservient to that purpose. Programs are not for consumption but for growth.

A shift from committee to team. We are being committee-ed and coun-cil-ed to death in our churches. In many of them, the primary way that a member actively participates in the church beyond attending worship is serving on a committee. Most of our volunteer time is then spent in plan-ning and policy-making functions that remain one step removed from ac-tual involvement in ministry. In reflections entitled "The Changing Shape of the Church," Ed White of the Alban Institute notes the trend "from an emphasis on *program* to an emphasis on *ministry:* Instead of preplanned programs that get organized and carried out according to a set pattern, there will be more willingness to approach the world with open hands and to respond to what one finds."[18] As groups come together and discover their context, calling, and gifts, a ministry team forms with an energy never achieved by a committee.

A shift from being clergy dominated to being laity oriented. Ed White adds this shift to his list of trends: "From an emphasis on *professional Chris-tians* (clergy), who are center stage in the gathered church, to *Christian professionals* who are ministering in the world and in the workplace: It is the laity who will be the 'leaven in the lump' as agents of renewal in our failing institutions."[19] When the primary involvement of members is sitting on planning and policy committees, is it any wonder that they look to staff to implement programs and that staff have difficulty "giving ministry away," as Bruce Larsen is fond of putting it?

A shift from recruitment to mission. The two words move in opposite directions. Recruitment is the orientation inherent in the vendor church, which tries to attract people to be regular and committed consumers of its programs and services — that is, to be satisfied customers. Mission moves in an opposite direction. It moves outward. It is concerned about giving the gospel away, not getting people in.

A shift from entrepreneur to missionary. In recent years it has become fashionable to advocate a shift in pastoral style "from maintenance to mis-sion." Among other things, leaders are challenged to move from being

18. Edward A. White, "The Changing Shape of the Church," *Presbyterian Outlook*, 23 March 1992, p. 6.

19. White, "The Changing Shape of the Church," p. 6.

passive and responsive to being active and proactive. Based on a vendor model, this new "mission leader" becomes an entrepreneur instead of a mere manager. Yet if we are to move beyond the vendor model, we need to be clearer about what a missionary leader is. A true missionary leader is one who forms the kind of community that embodies and represents in its life, deeds, and words the reign of God that Jesus announced is here.

A New Sense of Viability

Finally, we will need to revise our notions of viability, especially as we apply them to the small church and to new church development. What do we think makes a church viable? By what standard do we determine what a *real* church is? Does viability assume certain levels of financial resources? Does it assume a certain set of programs? Does it assume paid, professional leadership? According to the vendor model of the church, the answer to each question is yes, and this is where the greatest stress is felt in our churches. It is felt especially in our smaller churches, where a sense of inferiority sets in when they cannot support a full-time pastor or sustain a full array of services and programs. It is felt in new church developments where there is pressure to become a "*real* church" in terms of facilities, programs, staffing, and budget.

Consider the way we approach new church development in many of our mainline denominations. Operating with a vendor notion of the church, we ask the marketing question: Where will a church of our type (brand?) have a good chance of succeeding? What would happen if we asked instead the mission question: Where is there a need for the healing presence of a Christian community? The marketing question is asked in order to determine cost-effectiveness. The mission question invariably leads to something that is more costly than effective. But is this not the nature of our calling? Pondering the difference between these two questions, we may find new ways to think about small and new churches. Pondering the difference, we may even find innovations in small and new churches that will help us re-form all of our churches as missionary communities.

Representing the Reign of God

1998

This is a time for a dramatically new vision. The current predicament of churches in North America requires more than a mere tinkering with long-assumed notions about the identity and mission of the church. Instead, as many knowledgeable observers have noted, there is a need for reinventing or rediscovering the church in this new kind of world.[1]

Two things have become quite clear to those who care about the church and its mission. On the one hand, the churches of North America have been dislocated from their prior social role of chaplain to the culture and society and have lost their once-privileged positions of influence. Religious life in general and the churches in particular have increasingly been relegated to the private spheres of life. Too readily, the churches

---

1. In the current discussion, one finds phrases like "once and future church," transition from "churched-culture local congregations to mission outposts," or visions of a phoenix-like church rising from the ashes in new forms of church that will grow "up from the grassroots." See Peter C. Hodgson, *Revisioning the Church: Ecclesial Freedom in the New Paradigm* (Philadelphia: Fortress, 1988); Lynne and Bill Hybels, *Rediscovering Church: The Story and Vision of Willow Creek Community Church* (Grand Rapids: Zondervan, 1995); Loren B. Mead, *The Once and Future Church: Reinventing the Congregation for a New Mission Frontier* (Bethesda: Alban Institute, 1991); Kennon L. Callahan, *Effective Church Leadership: Building on the Twelve Keys* (San Francisco: Harper & Row, 1990); E. Dixon Junkin, "Up from the Grassroots: The Church in Transition," in George R. Hunsberger and Craig Van Gelder, eds., *The Church between Gospel and Culture: The Emerging Mission in North America* (Grand Rapids: Eerdmans, 1996), pp. 308-18.

This essay first appeared in the collaboratively written book *Missional Church* and was the chapter for which the present author had drafting responsibility.

have accepted this as their proper place.[2] At the same time, the churches have become so accommodated to the American way of life that they are now domesticated, and it is no longer obvious what justifies their existence as particular communities. The religious loyalties that churches seem to claim and the social functions that they actually perform are at odds with each other. Discipleship has been absorbed into citizenship.[3]

The churches have a great opportunity in these circumstances, however. The same pressures that threaten the continued survival of some churches, disturb the confidence of others, and devalue the meaning of them all can actually be helpful in providing an opening for new possibilities. Emerging into view on the far side of the church's long experience of Christendom is a wide vista of potential for the people of God in the postmodern and post-Christian world of North America. The present is a wildly opportune moment for churches to find themselves and to put on the garments of their calling, their vocation.

The Chinese character for signifying the idea of "crisis" combines two other characters, the one for "danger" and the other for "opportunity." Crisis is made of both, and so too is the current situation of the church. Dangers lurk on all sides for churches, but probably the greatest dangers lie within. Long-established routines and long-held notions have a strong hold on any community, and a church is no exception. These routines and notions constitute a way of seeing what the church is and what it is for and in turn inform how a church operates from day to day. Such assumed patterns are brought into question, however, when the church recognizes that it has been demoted from its prior social importance and may have accommodated away something of its soul. The church must then ask, Are our structures and our assumptions about the church's nature and purpose no longer suited to the time and place in which we currently live? Might it be that both our organization and presuppositions have been dislodged from their moorings in the biblical message?

These are difficult questions for the church of any age and place because they involve the complicated calling of the church to both relevance and faithfulness. The church may fit well into its social environment, but unwarranted accommodation may cause it to lose touch with its biblical warrant. Or the church may adhere too strictly to scriptural forms of expressing its faith that were intelligible to the cultures of biblical times, and

2. See Lesslie Newbigin, *Foolishness to the Greeks: The Gospel and Western Culture* (Grand Rapids: Eerdmans, 1986); Walter Brueggemann, *Disciplines of Readiness* (Louisville: Theology and Worship Unit, Presbyterian Church [USA], n.d.).

3. Stanley Hauerwas and William H. Willimon, *Resident Aliens: Life in the Christian Colony* (Nashville: Abingdon, 1989).

in the process neglect to translate the biblical warrant into an incarnation relevant to the church's current time and place. The struggle to be both faithful and relevant is constant for every church. It is the church's calling to embody the gospel's "challenging relevance."[4]

How is the church to give relevant expression and faithful embodiment to the gospel? The present crisis over the church's identity and mission is wrapped up in that question.

A Place or a People?

One way to illustrate and pose this question for the church today is to contrast the church's notion of itself in terms dictated by a functional Christendom with newer biblical and theological rumblings in this century concerning the church's nature. In lectures in 1991, shortly before his untimely death, mission theologian David Bosch of South Africa put it this way.[5] The churches shaped by the Reformation were left with a view of the church that was not directly intended by the Reformers, but nevertheless resulted from the way that they spoke about the church. Those churches came to conceive the church as "a place where certain things happen." The Reformers emphasized as the "marks of the true church" that such a church exists wherever the gospel is rightly preached, the sacraments rightly administered, and (they sometimes added) church discipline exercised. In their time, these emphases may have been profoundly missional since they asserted the authority of the Bible for the church's life and proclamation as well as the importance of making that proclamation accessible to all people. But over time, these "marks" narrowed the church's definition of itself toward a "place where" idea. This understanding was not so much articulated as presumed. It was never officially stated in a formal creed but was so ingrained in the churches' practice that it became dominant in the churches' self-understanding.

This perception of the church gives little attention to the church as a communal entity or presence, and it stresses even less the community's role as the bearer of missional responsibility throughout the world, both near

---

4. See Lesslie Newbigin, "Christ and the Cultures," *Scottish Journal of Theology* 31, no. 1 (1978): 1-22; and *The Open Secret: Sketches for a Missionary Theology*, rev. ed. (Grand Rapids: Eerdmans, 1995), chap. 9.

5. These six lectures were given by Bosch in April of 1991 at Western Theological Seminary in Holland, Michigan. There are audio and videotapes of the lectures in the seminary's library collection.

and far away. "Church" is conceived in this view as *the place where* a Christianized civilization gathers for worship, and *the place where* the Christian character of the society is cultivated. Increasingly, this view of the church as a "place where certain things happen" located the church's self-identity in its organizational forms and its professional class, the clergy who perform the church's authoritative activities. Popular grammar captures it well: you "go to church" much the same way you might go to a store. You "attend" a church, the way you attend a school or theater. You "belong to a church" as you would to a service club with its programs and activities.

This view corresponds well to the basic notion of mission that has existed under Christendom. On the one hand, the Reformers and their immediate successors believed that the commission Jesus left with the apostles — to disciple the nations — was fulfilled in the first century. Therefore it was no longer required of the church. The colonial expansion of European nations raised new questions about this belief as the churches of Europe encountered peoples who had never heard the gospel. When the question of evangelizing these peoples began to press itself, another strongly held belief of the time came into question as well. In Christendom Europe, civil magistrates were obligated to ensure the spiritual well-being of all citizens of their realm, so it was natural to assume that they would bear the same role vis-à-vis the new peoples brought under their dominion. This arrangement began to break down when voluntary missionary societies emerged. Many of those societies were ultimately adopted into the life of the churches, but mission continued to be conceived as something that happens at a great physical or social distance. The missionary movement throughout the nineteenth century altered little the western churches' self-conception as a place where certain things happened.

In the twentieth century, Bosch went on to say, this self-perception gave way to a new understanding of the church as *a body of people sent on a mission.* Unlike the previous notion of the church as an entity located in a facility or in an institutional organization and its activities, now the church is being reconceived as a community, a gathered people, brought together by a common calling and vocation to be a *sent people.* This understanding arose out of global reflections on the church's nature particularly in the light of the worldwide missionary movements of the previous several centuries and the fruit of that work in the existence of new churches throughout the world. From the mid-twentieth century on, biblical and theological foundations for such a communal and missional view of the church have blossomed.

Reflections among numerous missionary agencies and denominational mission boards following World War II underscored this perspective. During the middle of the twentieth century, the colonial worlds of the European nations were dismantled, and newly independent nations arose throughout the so-called Third World. Those churches previously called "younger churches" now pressed toward their own independence from the missions and churches of the West. A now-global church recognized that the church of any place bears missional calling and responsibility for its own place as well as for distant places. The church of every place, it realized, is a mission-sending church, and the place of every church is a mission-receiving place.

As a result of these developments, a shift from an *ecclesiocentric* (church-centered) view of mission to a *theocentric* (God-centered) one took place. Mission as a church-centered enterprise characterized mission thinking earlier in the twentieth century. Mission had been considered to be activities arising out of the church with an aim to extend the church or plant it in new places. The church sent the mission out and defined its character. The expansion of the church into new locales was thought to be its guiding goal. In many respects this shift represented an advance for the church because it acknowledged a global sense of mission. But this approach tended to reinforce the dichotomy between the churches of the West and the so-called younger churches planted in other parts of the world.

By mid-century, the emphasis in mission thought shifted toward a *theocentric* approach that, in contrast, stressed the mission of God *(missio Dei)* as the foundation for the mission of the church. The church became redefined as the community spawned by the mission of God and gathered up into that mission. The church was coming to understand that in any place it is a community sent by God. "Mission" is not something the church does, a part of its total program. No, the church's essence is missional, for the calling and sending action of God forms its identity. Mission is founded on the mission of God in the world, rather than the church's effort to extend itself.

Theocentric mission theology recovered the trinitarian character of mission. As Lesslie Newbigin indicated at the time, missionary practice must be grounded in the person and work of Christ, seeded by "trust in the reality and power of the Holy Spirit," and rooted in a practical faith that discerns "God's fatherly rule in the events of secular history, . . . in the revolutionary changes which are everywhere taking place in the life of the world."[6]

6. Lesslie Newbigin, *Trinitarian Faith and Today's Mission* (Richmond: John Knox, 1964), p. 77.

Recent theology has made a similar rediscovery by bringing to light the implications of the Trinity for ecclesiology. It has recognized that the *perichoresis,* or interpenetration, among the persons of the Trinity reveals that "the nature of God is communion." From this point of view, the church is learning that it is called to be a "finite echo or bodying forth of the divine personal dynamics," "a temporal echo of the eternal community that God is."[7]

What is not yet fully developed in these fresh approaches to trinitarian doctrines is the missional implication for ecclesiology. What does it mean that the church bears the stamp of the "eternal community" that God is *and* reflects the eternal mutual "sending" that characterizes that divine communion? Nowhere is the latter characteristic of the church so fully evident as in the biblical account of Jesus Christ. Jesus can and does say he will send his disciples the Advocate, the Spirit of truth (John 15:26), but it was that very same Spirit who baptized Jesus, led him in the wilderness while he was facing temptation, and filled him with power when he began his itinerant preaching (Luke 3:22; 4:1, 14). Jesus proclaimed that this Spirit rested on him and anointed him to preach good news (Luke 4:17-21). This mutuality in sending or "interprocession," if we may call it that, marks the divine communion as a communion of mission, and this in turn leaves its mark on the church.[8]

One more point of theological recovery that is particularly relevant to this discussion involves the importance of the fourth of the *notae,* or characteristics, of the church mentioned in the Nicene-Constantinopolitan Creed (AD 381). This creed affirms belief in "one, holy, catholic, and apostolic church." The last-mentioned distinctive of the church, "apostolic," asserts the church's missional vocation. As Jürgen Moltmann has put it, "The historical church must be called 'apostolic' in a double sense: its gospel and its doctrine are founded on the testimony of the first apostles, the eyewitnesses of the risen Christ, and it exists in the carrying out of the apostolic proclamation, the missionary charge. The expression 'apostolic' therefore

7. Colin E. Gunton, *The Promise of Trinitarian Theology* (Edinburgh: T. & T. Clark, 1991), quotations from pp. 72, 74, and 79, respectively; see also Leonardo Boff, *Trinity and Society,* trans. Paul Burns (Maryknoll, NY: Orbis, 1988), especially pp. 232-42.

8. See also Colin E. Gunton, *The One, the Three and the Many: God, Creation and the Culture of Modernity* (Cambridge: Cambridge University Press, 1993); Catherine Mowry LaCugna, *God for Us: The Trinity and Christian Life* (San Francisco: HarperSanFrancisco, 1991); Jürgen Moltmann, *The Trinity and the Kingdom: The Doctrine of God,* trans. Margaret Kohl (San Francisco: Harper & Row, 1981).

denotes both the church's foundation and its commission."[9] In a recent and important study of the understanding of the word *apostolic* within the early church, Robert Scudieri concludes the same: "The church is apostolic not just because it represents the apostles' teaching, but because it re-presents Christ."[10]

A People Sent or a Vendor of Religion?

This rethinking of the nature of God, church, and mission would appear to be a promising development if it were in fact evident in the operative style of today's churches or in the conceptions that govern them. But it is not. Indeed, the grammar commonly used to refer to or ask about the church still carries the heavy baggage of being a "place where certain things happen." We ask, for instance, "Where do you go to church?" "Where is your church?" "Did you go to church last Sunday?" Indeed, even when not referring to a tangible building, we tend to relate "church" to a meeting or activity, a set of programs, or an organizational structure. Only with awkwardness would one talk about being "part of a church."

In North America, this "place where" orientation manifests itself in a particular form. Both members and those outside the church expect the church to be *a vendor of religious services and goods*.

It is not hard to see how this expectation arose in North American life. The social order in modern societies was defined by the fact that freely choosing, autonomous individuals decided out of rational self-interest to enter into a social contract to construct a progressive society. Also defined in this way were the various social entities within society, including the church. The church as one such voluntary association lives off the willingness of its members to remain in it. Gaining the loyalty of members and retaining that loyalty takes priority in a voluntary association. The development of rational social organization in modern societies added another element to this characteristic of social life. Models of order, efficiency, progress, and growth were increasingly applied to the social order, and with this application the orderly management of social organizations by rational

9. Jürgen Moltmann, *The Church in the Power of the Spirit: A Contribution to Messianic Ecclesiology*, trans. Margaret Kohl (New York: Harper & Row, 1977), p. 358.

10. Robert J. Scudieri, *The Apostolic Church: One, Holy, Catholic and Missionary* (Fort Wayne: Lutheran Society for Missiology, 1995), p. 28.

technique became the rule. This naturally focused attention on the division of labor around the tasks of planning, organizing, structuring, and managing in a social entity conceived to be a machinelike, rational whole. In such an organizational configuration the individual was both manipulable part and capable master, and managing the organization became the equivalent of being the church.

Parallel with the rise of the "member as volunteer" and the "church as organization" was the impact of economic developments. Recent scholarship in the sociology of religion has brought to light how this aspect shaped the church's life. In *The Churching of America, 1776-1990: Winners and Losers in Our Religious Economy,* Roger Finke and Rodney Stark argue that the choice made early on in the United States not to have an established religion meant that an economic understanding of religious life and practice was inevitable. They contend that "where religious affiliation is a matter of choice, religious organizations must compete for members and . . . the 'invisible hand' of the marketplace is as unforgiving of ineffective religious firms as it is of their commercial counterparts. . . . Religious economies are like commercial economies in that they consist of a market made up of a set of current and potential customers and a set of firms seeking to serve that market." Indeed, they suggest that it is appropriate to use "economic concepts such as markets, firms, market penetration, and segmented markets to analyze the success and failure of religious bodies." In their view, then, the clergy are the church's sales representatives, religious doctrines its products, and evangelization practices its marketing techniques.[11]

This model has a ring of truth about it. It describes only too well assumptions about membership, program, structure, success, and purpose that give shape to today's church culture, "the way we do things around here." It certainly illumines the current circumstance in which the churches live, a pervasive religious consumerism driven by the quest to meet personally defined religious needs. It also explains the heavy concentration of church efforts to produce and promote programs, and it corresponds with the emphasis in one stream of literature flowing out of the church growth movement. That stream has accepted the commercial image without ques-

11. Roger Finke and Rodney Stark, *The Churching of America, 1776-1990: Winners and Losers in Our Religious Economy* (New Brunswick: Rutgers University Press, 1992), p. 17. These authors represent a "new paradigm" for the analysis of religious behavior in North America. They posit a "rational-choice" theory of religion by applying economic theories in a "market perspective" to religious phenomena. The work cited is typical of this approach.

tion by commending strategies for effectively and successfully "marketing your church."[12]

But here is the rub. Does this image of church correspond to the cluster of images found for the church in the New Testament? Does it correlate with New Testament speech about the nature and purposes of the church? At the very least, this producer-consumer model separates its notion of church (a religious firm producing and marketing religious products and services) from its members (potential and hopefully committed customers consuming those products and services). Members are ultimately distanced in this model from their own communal calling to be a body of people sent on a mission. The gap between these two notions is great, and it is in the transformation from the one to the other that the present challenge before the churches finds focus.

Rehearing the Gospel

Questions about the church's life that are this fundamental require a fresh hearing of the gospel. They demand that we return to the biblical rendering of the gospel and contemplate its vision of the church against the backdrop of recent social and cultural trends. A fresh hearing of the gospel is an effort to get back to roots in order to be clear about the essence of what it means to be the church. Hans Küng contends that the essence is in the church's "origins in the gospel." It is in the good news told in the New Testament, news that is continually spawning the church in every time and place. The church's essence, he points out, is always embodied in some tangible, visible form that is shaped by its particular time in history and its place in some specific human society. This is why we should not be surprised that the church's forms are diverse and variable across time and space. But what explains the church — what makes it the *church* — is that its life is birthed by the Holy Spirit as the Spirit gives hearing and response to the gospel.[13]

To say that the church's essence is found in its origins in the gospel is not, however, to say we only look back to the church's historical beginnings. The gospel, centered profoundly for Jesus in the announcement that the reign of God is at hand, is eschatological in character. It pulls back the veil

12. E.g., George Barna, *A Step-By-Step Guide to Church Marketing: Breaking Ground for the Harvest* (Ventura, CA: Regal, 1992).

13. Hans Küng, *The Church* (Garden City, NY: Image, 1967), pp. 22-24.

on the coming reign of God, thereby revealing the horizon of the world's future. The gospel portrays the coming of Jesus, and particularly his death and resurrection, as the decisive, truly eschatological event in the world's history. Therefore a community with origins in the gospel is "an eschatological community of salvation." As such, it "comes from the preaching of the reign of God — the reign of God is its beginning and its foundation. And it moves towards the revealed consummation of the reign of God — the reign of God is its goal, its limitation, its judgment." The church is defined by its origins in a gospel that casts a vision of its destiny that always draws it forward.[14]

This definition suggests for the church a lifestyle of continual conversion as it hears and responds to the gospel over and over again.[15] The church is constantly being reevangelized, and by virtue of that it is always being constituted and formed as the church. The essence of what it means to be the church arises perpetually from the church's origins in the gospel: it is in every moment being *originated* by the Holy Spirit as it hears the gospel and is *oriented* by "the present reign of Christ in which the coming completed reign of God . . . is revealed and becomes effective in the present."[16] This is true whatever the time or place, but it becomes especially crucial at times of great social and cultural shifts, both those involving the church's own social position and those in the surrounding context itself. Such transformations raise questions about how the church will fit in its altered setting, and these questions lead ultimately to queries about whether the church's forms reflect an authentic hearing of the gospel and a genuine sharing in its vision.

What exactly is the gospel, then? Identifying the gospel is both simple and challenging. No culture-free expression of the gospel exists, nor could it. The church's message, the gospel, is inevitably articulated in linguistic and cultural forms particular to its own place and time. Thus a rehearing of the gospel can be vulnerable to the "gospels" that we may tend to read back into the New Testament renderings of it. The first tellings of the gospel in Scripture themselves have a richly varied quality. They are as culturally particular as our own. Nevertheless, they are the root narrative of God's action in Jesus Christ for the salvation of the world, and as such, the church's originating message. It is of the essence of the church to root itself in what those first tellings portray of the character, actions, and purposes of God.

14. Küng, *The Church*, pp. 116-33, quotations from pp. 116 and 133, respectively.
15. For a full treatment of this important theme, see Darrell L. Guder, *The Continuing Conversion of the Church: Evangelization as the Heart of Ministry* (Grand Rapids: Eerdmans, 2000).
16. Küng, *The Church*, p. 126.

Good News: The Reign of God Is at Hand

The gospel is Jesus himself. The New Testament's Gospels narrate the life, death, and resurrection of Jesus as the action of God that both reveals God's passion for the world and achieves God's purpose for that world. Other depictions of the gospel in the New Testament affirm the same thing, whether in Luke's reports in Acts of the early churches' communication of the gospel, or in the letters and literature that constitute the churches' reflections on its significance. Long anticipated in the Old Testament's portraits of the saving and covenanting urges of the God who made the world and all that is in it, Jesus is recognized throughout the New Testament as the incarnate Son of God, the anointed Redeemer ("Messiah" from the Hebrew, "Christ" from the Greek), and the Ruler and Judge of the world.

If this is true, however, we must also hear what Jesus himself said, what he himself called the "good news." The churches of the New Testament proclaimed Jesus as the Christ, the reigning Lord, by virtue of his crucifixion and resurrection. In this sense their gospel was *about* Jesus. But whatever they proclaimed about Jesus was in concert with the spirit and substance of Jesus' teaching and preaching. Their gospel was not only *about* Jesus — it was also the gospel *of* Jesus, the gospel that he preached. This was so because the Jesus whom they announced as the risen Christ of God, the living Lord of the nations, embodied the message spoken from his lips. Jesus' good news that the reign of God is at hand is clothed with meaning by his continuing presence as the risen, reigning, and glorified Lord. Believing *in* Jesus Christ also means believing Jesus Christ about the reign of God.

Proclaiming a gospel about Christ that is not shaped by the gospel Jesus preached distorts the gospel by proclaiming only part of its meaning. The absence of the gospel Jesus preached in the gospel the church has preached has woefully impoverished the church's sense of missional identity. A rehearing of the gospel at this time in the history of the North American churches requires special attention to Jesus' own announcement of the good news.

What did this one who is the good news have to say when he announced the good news? What was the gospel he preached? What was the message in his evangelizing? The answer is not hard to find. It comes in quick succession from the pages of the biblical Gospels. The earliest one, Mark, sets the stage in its opening lines: the theme will be "the beginning of the good news of Jesus Christ, the Son of God" (1:1). Thereafter, in the briefest of introductions, John the Baptist offers a trumpetlike fanfare for Jesus, a descending dove (the Spirit) anoints him for his mission, and a voice from heaven validates him. Then Jesus is heard in tones that would permeate all his preaching and teaching: "Jesus came to Galilee, proclaiming the good news of God, and saying, 'The time is fulfilled, and the kingdom of God has come near; repent, and believe in the good news'" (1:14-15). For Mark, as for Matthew and Luke after him, this fundamental announcement was emblematic of all Jesus taught. Here lies the central and guiding theme of the message he was compelled to announce. One New Testament scholar has said what scholarship in general has accepted:

> The central aspect of the teaching of Jesus was that concerning the Kingdom of God. Of this there can be no doubt. . . . Jesus appeared as one who proclaimed the Kingdom; all else in his message and ministry serves a function in relation to that proclamation and derives its meaning from it. The challenge to discipleship, the ethical teaching, the disputes about oral tradition or ceremonial law, even the pronouncement of forgiveness of sins and the welcoming of the outcast in the name of God — all these are to be understood in the context of the Kingdom proclamation or they are not to be understood at all.[17]

It is important to note here that this central theme shaped for Jesus the sense of his mission as well as the mantle of that mission that he passed to his followers. Luke, who reports the beginning of Jesus' preaching by describing his maiden sermon in his hometown synagogue in Nazareth, notices the hold this theme has on Jesus' mind. The Nazareth incident itself involves the Isaiah text about the anticipated "year of the Lord's favor" and a messianic appointment by the Spirit of one who will proclaim its arrival: good news to the poor, release to the captives, sight to the blind, freedom to the oppressed. Surely this is a portrait of the reign of God coming! About this Isaiah text, Jesus said simply, "Today this scripture has been fulfilled in your hearing" (4:21). As the narrative of Jesus' ministry unfolds, the intent of that ministry is clearly identified. Healings among the people of Capernaum lead them to cling to Jesus and urge him to remain with them. "But he said to them, 'I must proclaim the good news of the kingdom of God to the other cities also; for I was sent for this purpose'" (4:43). Jesus' commitment to do and say only what his Father had assigned him, so in evidence

17. Norman Perrin, *Rediscovering the Teaching of Jesus* (New York: Harper & Row, 1967), p. 54.

elsewhere in the Gospels, focused his mission on this announcement of the good news that the reign of God is at hand.

It was this message that Jesus placed on the lips of disciples whom he sent out to share in the fulfillment of his mission. "As you go, proclaim the good news, 'The kingdom of heaven has come near'" (Matt. 10:7). The same was also embedded in his forecast of the mission that the whole church would inherit: "And this good news of the kingdom will be proclaimed throughout the world, as a testimony to all the nations; and then the end will come" (Matt. 24:14).

The language and emphasis of John's Gospel move in directions different from those of the Synoptic Gospels. But his Gospel nevertheless corresponds with the portraits of the other three by showing Jesus' mission as centered on the presence of the reign of God. As Albert Curry Winn has noted, John portrays Jesus as one who possessed a "sense of having been sent." His will is not his own, but God's. His words are not his own, but God's. His works are not his own, but God's. His very life depends on the Sender.[18] Jesus declares to Pilate, "My kingdom is not from this world. . . . My kingdom is not from here" (John 18:36). Throughout the Gospel of John, what is at stake is whether one believes, and belief or lack of it is linked with whether one can "see" or "enter" the kingdom of God (3:3, 5). What is announced is that "God so loved the world that he gave his only Son" and that God sent the Son "in order that the world might be saved through him" (3:16-17). The kingdom of God and the world are at odds in the portrait offered by John's Gospel. John's use of the term *world* refers, for the most part, to "human society as it is structured in opposition to Christ and to the followers of Christ," just as it is also "opposed to God" and God's rightful authority.[19]

What Is This Reign of God?

Exactly what is this reign of God, then, that Jesus so routinely announces? All the Synoptic Gospels convey the sense that the reign of God has a certain indefinable quality in Jesus' own teaching. Always a mystery yet an open secret, it was best passed on by way of parables, whose intent was to reveal and to hide in the same breath.

---

18. Albert Curry Winn, *A Sense of Mission: Guidance from the Gospel of John* (Philadelphia: Westminster, 1981), pp. 30-34.

19. Winn, *A Sense of Mission*, pp. 69-70.

A definitive answer to the question, What is the reign of God? cannot be given. But we can at least sketch some of its contours by listening to the Old Testament's prophetic forecasts of the coming day of God and the prophets' expectations of God's intended future for the world. In lectures given in the early 1980s, philosopher Arthur Holmes summarized that prophetic vision as *shalom*. It envisions a world characterized by peace, justice, and celebration. *Shalom,* the overarching vision of the future, means "peace," but not merely peace as the cessation of hostilities. Instead, shalom envisions the full prosperity of a people of God living under the covenant of God's demanding care and compassionate rule. In the prophetic vision, peace such as this comes hand in hand with justice. Without justice, there can be no real peace, and without peace no real justice. Indeed, only in a social world full of a peace grounded in justice can there come the full expression of joy and celebration.[20]

It is striking to note, in this light, Paul's brief passing notes about the character of the reign of God. During an extended conversation about diverse opinions on dietary practices, he comments, "For the kingdom of God is not food and drink, but righteousness [justice] and peace and joy in the Holy Spirit" (Rom. 14:17). The prophetic vision is there, joined now to the presence of the Holy Spirit, who enables it.

The reign of God most certainly arises as God's mission to reconcile the creation accomplished in the death and resurrection of Jesus. "In Christ, God was reconciling the world to himself" (2 Cor. 5:19). "If anyone is in Christ, there is a new creation" (2 Cor. 5:17). "But each in his own order: Christ the first fruits, then at his coming those who belong to Christ. Then comes the end, when he hands over the kingdom to God the Father, after he has destroyed every ruler and every authority and power" (1 Cor. 15:23-24). Ruling by way of a cross and a resurrection, God thwarts the powers of sin and death that distort the creation once good at its beginning. The future rule of God breaks in ahead of time as a harbinger of the world's future to be fully and finally reconciled to God.

Where Did We Lose It?

It is hotly debated just when and how the church lost its sense of this gospel of the reign of God, with the result that its message ceased to orient

20. Arthur Holmes, the Staley Lectures, Belhaven College, Jackson, Mississippi.

the church's own life and witness. Some say it was quite early because the church's formation itself was a reversal of the kingdom. This view is hard to sustain, especially since it was the earliest, emergent church that remembered and subsequently put into writing the gospel of Jesus, the proclaimer of the reign of God. Luke's account of the early church and the spread of its witness emphasizes how centered it was on this core announcement. Philip "was proclaiming the good news about the kingdom of God and the name of Jesus Christ" (Acts 8:12). Paul and Barnabas encouraged new disciples to continue in the faith: "It is through many persecutions that we must enter the kingdom of God" (14:22). Paul entered the synagogue in Ephesus and "spoke out boldly and argued persuasively about the kingdom of God" (19:8). His memoir would assert that there in Ephesus he had gone about "proclaiming the kingdom" (20:25). While under house arrest in Rome, he entertained visitors, both Jews and Gentiles, among whom he was "proclaiming the kingdom of God and teaching about the Lord Jesus Christ with all boldness and without hindrance" (28:23, 31). These comments and others show how central this announcement was in the early church's missional identity and message.

But it is not hard to see that at many times in the church's history this central affirmation of good news has suffered a pattern of omission or "eclipse," as Mortimer Arias has described it.[21] Two tendencies in the long history of Christendom help to explain this troublesome pattern. First, the church has tended to separate the news of the reign of God from God's provision for humanity's salvation. This separation has made salvation a private event by dividing "my personal salvation" from the advent of God's healing reign over all the world. Second, the church has also tended to envision itself in a variety of ways unconnected to what must be fundamental for it — its relation to the reign of God. If it was Jesus' announcement of the reign of God that first gathered the fledgling church into community, and

21. Mortimer Arias, *Announcing the Reign of God: Evangelization and the Subversive Memory of Jesus* (Philadelphia: Fortress, 1984), pp. 55-67. Arias argues that the "eclipse" is not adequately explained simply by noting that in place of the good news of the reign of God the church has proclaimed Jesus as King. These are not opposed to each other but are complementary. As one Latin American theologian has put it: "Kingdom of God and person of Jesus (in the Lukan conception) explain and fulfill each other, in such a way that we cannot speak of kingdom of God without Christ, or Christ without *basileia* (kingdom). . . . Christology is always oriented towards its frame of reference in the *basileia*" (Augustin del Agua Perez, "El Cumplimiento del Reino de Dios en la Misión de Jesús," *Estudios Biblicos* 38 [1979-80]: 292, quoted in translation by Arias, *Announcing the Reign of God,* p. 60).

if that church grew and matured around the way that reign found meaning and hope in his death and resurrection, then the church must always seek its definition with the reign of God in Christ as its crucial reference point.

The Reign of God as Missional Perspective

A significant recovery of "reign of God" or "kingdom of God" language has been evident within the field of biblical scholarship. To some extent, the same is true of church conversations about mission. But even when that is so, the use of such language in common church parlance tends not to be thought out very well. Typical Christian conversation on this subject speaks of "building" or "extending" the reign of God. These two ways of talking represent dominant and sometimes opposing ideologies in the North American churches. In both cases, the images of building or extending arise from the combined effects of a Christendom heritage of power and privilege, the Enlightenment's confidence in reason and social progress, and modern culture's dependence on managing life with pragmatic technique.

Those who imagine the church's role as "building" the reign of God may also use words like "establish," "fashion," or "bring about." The reign of God in this view is perceived as a social project. The church is sent out by God to achieve that project, to create it. This view tends to place the reign out there somewhere, where we go to construct it as its architects, contractors, carpenters, or day laborers.

Others say the church is sent to "extend" the reign of God. They speak in terms of "spreading," "growing," or "expanding" the reign of God. This treats the church's mission as a sales project. The church attempts to provide an expanded place where the reign of God may reside. Functionally, the church becomes the CEOs, promoters, or sales force for the reign of God.

But the grammar by which the New Testament depicts the reign of God cuts across the grain of these North American culture-bound ways of seeing things. The verbs *to build* and *to extend* are not found in the New Testament's grammar for the reign of God. The announcement of God's reign nowhere includes an invitation to go out and build it, nor to extend it. These are not New Testament ways of speaking about the reign of God.

The words most often used evoke quite a different spirit and, therefore, a very different missional identity and engagement. The New Testament employs the words *receive* and *enter*. They come at times intertwined in the text. "Truly I tell you, whoever does not receive the kingdom of God as a child will never enter it" (Luke 18:17).[22] In that same context Jesus notes how hard it is for those who have riches to *enter* the reign of God (vv. 24-25), and he assures the disciples that there is no one who has left mother or father, houses or land, for the gospel's sake, who will not *receive* one hundredfold (vv. 29-30).

These two verbs represent dominant image clusters embedded throughout the New Testament's discussion of the relationship between the people of God and the reign of God. Taken together they indicate the appropriate way for a community to live when it has been captured by the presence of God's reign.

For example, the reign of God is, first of all, a gift one receives. The reign of God is something taken to oneself. It is a gift of God's making, freely given. It calls for the simple, trusting act of receiving.

The reign of God is something that *has been* given. "Do not be afraid, little flock," says Jesus, "for it is your Father's good pleasure to *give* you the kingdom" (Luke 12:32). It is something, then, that one can possess now. "Blessed are you who are poor, for yours *is* the kingdom of God" (6:20). "Let the children come to me; do not stop them; for it is to such as these that the kingdom of God *belongs*" (Mark 10:14; cf. Luke 18:16).

While God's reign can "belong" to the children, as something already possessed, it is also described as a gift that awaits our possessing. It *will be inherited.* On the final day of judgment the Son of Man will say, "Come, you that are blessed of my Father, inherit the kingdom prepared for you from the foundation of the world" (Matt. 25:34). James refers to the poor as the "heirs of the kingdom" (2:5). The meek, Jesus said, "will inherit the earth" (Matt. 5:5). Paul in turn speaks of those who "will not inherit the kingdom of God" (1 Cor. 6:9-10; 15:50; Gal. 5:20; Eph. 5:5).

In addition to being a gift, the reign of God is equally a realm one

---

22. Here, as throughout, direct biblical quotations are from the New Revised Standard Version. That translation consistently uses "kingdom" to render the Greek word *basileia,* and so that word will appear within direct quotations of the Bible. But we have chosen to use "reign" throughout this text because it better captures, in our judgment, the dynamic meaning of *basileia,* which refers to the reigning itself and thus secondarily the realm incorporated under such reigning. "Kingdom," we believe, is too static, political, and archaic a word in our contemporary usage to do justice to the term, and it too easily identifies the *basileia* with a temporal entity like Christendom or particular structures of the church. As we will emphasize, the *basileia* and the church must never be divorced, but they also must never be equated. Similarly, the reign must never be separated from the One who reigns, the *basileus* at the heart of the *basileia.*

enters. Here the imagery is quite different, for the reign of God is cast as a domain into which one moves. It meets everyone with God's welcome and Jesus' invitation.

The reign of God is a realm — a space, an arena, a zone — that may be inhabited. Hence the biblical grammar for this reign uses the spatial preposition *in*. In the Sermon on the Mount, Jesus declares that some "will be called least *in* the kingdom of heaven" and others "called great *in* the kingdom of heaven" (Matt. 5:19). Likewise, Colossians 1:13 tells us that Jesus "has rescued us from the power of darkness and transferred us *into* the kingdom of his beloved Son."

This realm of the reign of God into which we are welcomed to enter is never equated with a particular human political regime. It is always, after all, the realm of the regime of God. But on the horizon lies the cosmic specter of the reign of God fulfilled. So the grammar of "inhabiting" the reign of God includes the prospect of a future destiny. The reign of God is an inhabiting for which we are destined. The question raised by many of the parables concerns who, in the end, shall enter. At the end time, the Lord's word to some will be, "Enter into the joy of your master" (Matt. 25:21, 23). Yet "not everyone who says to me, 'Lord, Lord,' will enter the kingdom of heaven, but only the one who does the will of my Father in heaven" (Matt. 7:21). Second Peter 1:11 affirms: "Entry into the eternal kingdom of our Lord and Savior Jesus Christ will be richly provided for you."[23]

Taking seriously these two images of the reign of God as a gift one receives and a realm one enters restrains our cultural instincts to think of the reign of God as something we achieve or enlarge. The biblical images of gift and realm are not without their own dangers, certainly. The former can lead to the presumptuous claim of owning the reign of God, and the latter to the prideful assertion of knowing ourselves to be "in" it. But if we follow faithfully the Bible's own use of these two images, we will discover that the images themselves provide the sharpest warnings against both presumption and pride. Jesus signals a great reversal in the imagery of giving and receiving, and welcoming and entering: "Therefore I tell you, the kingdom of God will be *taken away* from you and *given* to a people that produces the fruits of the kingdom" (Matt. 21:43). And to those who assumed themselves

23. Also in terms of this spatial image cluster, Jesus says to some, "You are not far from the kingdom of God" (Mark 12:34). Of others he says, "How hard it will be for those who have wealth to enter the kingdom of God" (10:23; cf. vv. 24-25; Luke 18:24-25; Matt. 19:23-24). Indeed, he says of some, "I tell you, unless your righteousness exceeds that of the scribes and Pharisees, you will never enter the kingdom of heaven" (Matt. 5:20).

rightfully first in line for entering God's reign, he warned: "Truly I tell you, the tax collectors and the prostitutes are going into the kingdom of God ahead of you" (21:31).

To summarize what we have learned, then, the reign of God is *given.* God's gift and welcome are its most striking and critical features. Biblical language about the reign of God also embraces the eschatological tension of God's reign being a present fact and an anticipated future. It suggests the need as well for decisive action now. The call to receive warns against the consequence of rejecting the gift. The invitation to enter casts a shadow on hesitation at the door.

Inherent within the two biblical images of gift and realm are the further issues of repentance and faith. Receiving and entering are actions that mark a turning from other hopes and loyalties that we may accumulate to a singular hope in the one true God. They mark a turning in faith from sinful rejections of God's rule as well as carefree disdain for God's mercy and care. Receiving and entering the reign of God are the ways we "turn to God from idols" (1 Thess. 1:9). This movement indicates that we are involved in an ongoing dynamic relationship with the divine reign and that we must distinguish between the reign of God and its responsive community, between God's reign and the church.

It is in these findings that any biblically rooted and contextually relevant sense of the calling of the church in North America must begin. Here is a far more dynamic sense of the church's identity and its mission in the world. This sense stands in bold contrast to the merely functional or activist notions of building or extending that have so prepossessed the church in North America. In this beginning place, one finds a more humble starting point for mission. It leads to the fresh insight that the first mission is always the internal mission: the church evangelized by the Holy Spirit again and again in the echoing word of Jesus inviting us to receive the reign of God and to enter it.

Here is also found a more dynamic image for every Christian's personal calling and discipleship. Daily life becomes a discipline of asking how one may move more squarely into the realm of God's reign and how one may welcome and receive it into the fabric of one's life this day more than ever before. Here as well one can find a more focused way of living together as the community of Christ. This point is especially crucial for churches that have suffered the loss of focus, the loss of a sense of what lies at the center, the loss of their soul.

Here, moreover, is a far more welcoming framework for evangelism.

Evangelism would move from an act of recruiting or co-opting those outside the church to an invitation of companionship. The church would witness that its members, like others, hunger for the hope that there is a God who reigns in love and intends the good of the whole earth. The community of the church would testify that they have heard the announcement that such a reign is coming, and indeed is already breaking into the world. They would confirm that they have heard the open welcome and received it daily, and they would invite others to join them as those who also have been extended God's welcome. To those invited, the church would offer itself to assist their entrance into the reign of God and to travel with them as co-pilgrims. Here lies a path for the renewal of the heart of the church and its evangelism.[24]

The Church and the Reign of God

It is obvious from all that has been said thus far that in Scripture and in the present the divine reign is distinguishable from *us*. It is something we can be in and something we can possess. But it is ultimately something other than who or what we are, and it can never be captive and owned by us in the sense of being controlled by us.

One of the two points where Matthew's Gospel mentions "church" *(ekklesia)* underscores this distinction and begins to establish the interrelationship between the reign of God and the church: "on this rock I will build my church," and then "I will give you the keys of the kingdom" (Matt. 16:18-19). Here it is clear that the church *(ekklesia)* and the reign of God *(basileia)* are separate conceptions, but also that the two are intimately bound together.

A clue to their relationship is present three chapters earlier amid the parables of the divine reign. In Jesus' interpretation of the parable of the weeds in the field, he says, "The field is the world, and the good seed are the children of the kingdom" (Matt. 13:38). At the end of the age, he goes on, "the Son of Man will send his angels, and they will collect out of his kingdom all causes of sin and all evildoers. . . . Then the righteous will shine like the sun in the kingdom of their Father" (vv. 41, 43). The messianic community is here construed to be the children of the divine reign, on the way

24. See William J. Abraham, *The Logic of Evangelism* (Grand Rapids: Eerdmans, 1989), for a compelling development of a theology of evangelistic ministry as "initiation into the kingdom."

to shining like the sun in that reign which is coming. In other words, the church is the offspring of the divine reign. It is its fruit, and therefore its evidence.

The church must not be equated with the reign of God. The church as a messianic community is both spawned by the reign of God and directed toward it. This is a different relationship from what at times has captured the church's thinking. The church has often presumed that the reign of God is within the church. The two have been regarded as synonyms. In this view, the church totally encompasses the divine reign. Therefore church extension or church growth is the equivalent of kingdom extension or kingdom growth, and the reign of God is coterminous with the people who embrace it through faith and gather together as the church. This view leads easily to the affirmation that there is no salvation outside the church. The church then sees itself as the fortress and guardian of salvation, perhaps even its author and benefactor, rather than its grateful recipient and guest.

The biblical portrait of the divine reign and the church does not allow such conclusions. The church always stands in a position of dependence on and humble service to the divine reign. The Dutch Reformed scholar Herman Ridderbos has stressed this point in *The Coming of the Kingdom:*

> *The* basileia [reign, kingdom] *is the great divine work of salvation in its fulfillment and consummation in Christ; the* ekklesia [church] *is the people elected and called by God and sharing in the bliss of the* basileia. Logically, the *basileia* ranks first, and not the *ekklesia.* . . . [The *basileia*] represents the all-embracing perspective, it denotes the consummation of all history, brings both grace and judgment, has cosmic dimensions, fills time and eternity. The *ekklesia* in all this is the people who in this great drama have been placed on the side of God in Christ by virtue of the divine election and covenant.[25]

But at the same time we must say with equal force that the reign of God must not be divorced from the church. The church is constituted by those who are entering and receiving the reign of God. It is where the children of the reign corporately manifest the presence and characteristic features of God's reign. The divine reign expresses itself in a unique, though not exhaustive or exclusive, fashion in the church.

25. Herman N. Ridderbos, *The Coming of the Kingdom,* ed. Raymond O. Zorn, trans. H. de Jongste (Philadelphia: Presbyterian & Reformed, 1962), p. 354.

The desire to distinguish between the two has sometimes led to views that ultimately divorce them. Such was the case in some ecumenical circles during the 1950s and 1960s when it was affirmed that "the church goes out into the reign of God." This trend of thought began with people like Hans Hoekendijk who were concerned that the church had for too long centered mission on the church itself, as though the church were both the initiator of the mission and the goal of it. Hoekendijk rightly insisted:

> The church cannot be more than a sign. She points away from herself to the Kingdom; she lets herself be used for and through the Kingdom in the oikoumene [the whole inhabited earth]. There is nothing that the church can demand for herself and can possess for herself (not an ecclesiology either). God has placed her in a living relationship to the Kingdom and to the oikoumene. The church exists only *in actu,* in the execution of the apostolate, i.e., in the proclamation of the gospel of the Kingdom to the world.[26]

As this view matured and was carried forward by Hoekendijk and others, however, it pictured the divine reign as essentially, if not totally, "out there" in the world. Consequently, the church was to go out to meet God. This vision of the church and its mission was most forcefully expressed by the report of a World Council of Churches study program entitled *The Church for Others* (1967). Lesslie Newbigin has summarized the thrust of that document:

> "Thinking about the Church should always begin by defining it as part of the world" (17). It is the world, not the Church, which "writes the agenda" (20-23), and the Church is not to be concerned about increasing its own membership (19). "Participation in God's mission is entering into partnership with God in history, because our knowledge of God in Christ compels us to affirm that God is working out his purpose in the midst of the world and its historical processes" (14). So "What else can the Churches do than recognize and proclaim what God is doing in the world" — in the emancipation of coloured races, the humanization of industrial relations, and so on?[27]

26. J. C. Hoekendijk, *The Church Inside Out,* ed. L. A. Hoedemaker and Pieter Tijmes, trans. Isaac C. Rottenberg (Philadelphia: Westminster, 1966), p. 43.
27. Lesslie Newbigin, "Recent Thinking on Christian Beliefs: VIII. Mission and Missions," *Expository Times* 88, no. 9 (1977): 261.

The instinct here to include the larger world within the scope of God's mission and reign is a good one. But the position stated here implies that the church is ultimately irrelevant to the mission of God or at least peripheral to it, since the reign of God is entirely located in the world. What is lost in this view is the church's reason for being a particular community, both distinct from the divine reign and yet spawned by it as its intended fruit and servant.

In contrast, Newbigin has affirmed a perspective that seeks to maintain the distinction between God's reign and the church but not break their connection:

> The . . . danger to be avoided is the separation of the Kingdom from the church. It is clear that they cannot and must not be confused, certainly not identified. But they must also not be separated. From the beginning the announcement of the Kingdom led to a summons to follow and so to the formation of a community. It is the community which has begun to taste (even only in foretaste) the reality of the Kingdom which can alone provide the hermeneutic of the message.[28]

When we ask then what positive model or understanding of the church would do justice to these two negative affirmations, we are led to capture the biblical sense of the church's calling and vocation this way: *the church represents the reign of God*. This is another way of rendering the fundamental New Testament notion of witness, but promises a fresh and holistic approach to viewing all of the church's life missionally. The word *represent* can carry two different senses, a passive one and an active one. The passive meaning indicates that one thing stands for another. When you have seen the one, you have known the other. An example of this form of representation would be the sentence, "The paper submitted to the professor represents the student's best effort." In contrast, the active meaning of *represent* indicates the way a person may be given authority to act on another's behalf or to care for another's interests, such as, "A lawyer represents her client," or "The secretary of state represents the president in this meeting." Both the passive and active meanings of "represent" are intended when it is said of the church that it represents the reign of God, and each adds particular force to the missional calling of the church.

The church represents the divine reign as its *sign and foretaste*. Themes

28. Lesslie Newbigin, *Sign of the Kingdom* (Grand Rapids: Eerdmans, 1980), p. 19.

woven into the fabric of the book of Ephesians illustrate this intended meaning. When the author speaks of the breaking down of the barriers between Jews and Gentiles (2:11ff.) that has resulted from the expansion of the gospel mission to the Gentile world, he states that this profound social change within the small community of Christians represents God's purpose for the world: "that he might create in himself one new humanity in place of the two, thus making peace" (2:15). The emerging multicultural church is here a foretaste of God's redeeming purpose for the world, which is the mystery now revealed: "that is, the Gentiles have become fellow heirs, members of the same body, and sharers in the promise in Christ Jesus through the gospel" (3:6). This point is even more explicit when the church is described as the sign of God's wisdom for the cosmos: "so that through the church the wisdom of God in its rich variety might now be made known to the rulers and authorities in the heavenly places" (3:10). As a sign represents something else and as a foretaste represents something yet to come, the church points away from itself to what God is going to complete. In this sense, the divine reign's otherness is guarded. The church must affirm that it is not identical with God's reign.

But the church also represents the divine reign as its *agent and instrument*. Here it represents that reign in an active sense. The church bears the divine reign's authority (the authority of the "keys," Matt. 16:19; and the authority of "forgiveness," as indicated in John 20:19-23). It engages in the divine reign's action (living in terms of the lordship of Jesus over all creation). For this reason, Paul may address Christians as "co-workers for the kingdom of God" (Col. 4:11) and consider them to be "suffering" for the reign of God (2 Thess. 1:5). The church is representative in the sense of an embassy ("ambassadors for Christ," 2 Cor. 5:20) of the divine reign.

By its very existence, then, the church brings what is hidden into view as sign and into experience as foretaste. At the same time, it also represents to the world the divine reign's character, claims, demands, and gracious gifts as its agent and instrument.

The Mission to Represent the Reign of God

In what forms should this representation take place? Just how does a community of people go about representing the reign of God among its neighbors near and far? The most likely location for an answer to these questions is the mission of Jesus. His mission, after all, represents the most direct and complete expression of God's mission in the world. Therefore the church's own mission must take its cues from the way God's mission unfolded in the sending of Jesus into the world for its salvation. In Jesus' way of carrying out God's mission, we discover that the church is to represent God's reign as its community, its servant, and its messenger.[29]

Representing the Reign of God as Its Community

Jesus believed it was his mission to embody the reign of God by living under its authority. He was the willing subject of God's reign. His baptism by John and anointing by the Spirit placed him under covenant obligations and promises. He claimed the role of fulfilling all righteousness. Therefore he bore the same covenant obligations Israel had borne, but fulfilled them as Israel never had.

This is the point of Jesus' temptations in the wilderness. It is not by accident that Jesus responds to each temptation presented by Satan with words from the Deuteronomic recapitulation of the covenant. In effect he was saying, "Here are the rules under which I am to live. I will abide by them." The test was whether he would keep covenant, whether he would live in ultimate trust and dependence on God, and whether he would give ultimate loyalty and obedience to God. The reign of God was present in a radically new way in Jesus because he lived trustingly and loyally under the gracious rule of his Father as none had lived before.

The church shares this calling with Jesus. In the church's case, though,

---

29. This triad, which emerges from Scripture, has constantly surfaced in the church's recent thinking about its mission. This was particularly the case in the 1950s when the experience of the modern missionary movement led Hans Hoekendijk and Hendrik Kraemer to articulate their threefold sense of the church's mission as *kerygma, diakonia,* and *koinonia.* The 1961 New Delhi Assembly of the World Council of Churches used the themes of witness, service, and unity to signal the three strands that had converged in the formulation of the Council (International Missionary Council, Life and Work, and Faith and Order). The Vatican II document *Lumen Gentium* portrays the church using the images of prophet, king, and priest. In *The Mustard Seed Conspiracy* (Waco: Word, 1981), Tom Sine speaks of the mission as words of love, deeds of love, and life of love. The book *Who in the World?* ed. Clifford Christians, Earl J. Schipper, and Wesley Smedes (Grand Rapids: Eerdmans, 1972), presented a report of a Christian Reformed Church conference that organized the church's mission around the truth (message), the life (community), and the way (servant). Darrell L. Guder talks about being the witness, doing the witness, and saying the witness in *Be My Witnesses: The Church's Mission, Message, and Messengers* (Grand Rapids: Eerdmans, 1985).

its vocation is corporate, not individual. Jesus, the one who represented Israel, is now represented by the new Israel, the church. Like Jesus, the church is to embody the reign of God by living under its authority. We live as the covenant community, a distinctive community spawned by God's reign to show forth its tangible character in human, social form.

Before the church is called to do or say anything, it is called and sent to be the unique community of those who live under the reign of God. The church displays the firstfruits of the forgiven and forgiving people of God who are brought together across the rubble of dividing walls that have crumbled under the weight of the cross. It is the harbinger of the new humanity that lives in genuine community, a form of companionship and wholeness that humanity craves.

What the church identifies as true about itself because of Christ, it also knows to be far from true about itself in its present experience. Yet it is precisely this affirmation made by Christ concerning who the church is that moves it to actualize in practice what it believes true.[30] Believing itself to be one in the "unity of the Spirit" (Eph. 4:3), the church knows God has sent it into the pursuit of the "unity of the faith" (4:13).

Of course, God delights in having a people who are one in love, and God's people enjoy the freedom of being that particular people. But there is another reason for this mission of being the community of the reign of God. "You are the light of the world," Jesus said (Matt. 5:14). We are a noticed and watched people. The genuineness of our identification as the disciples of Jesus is observed only in our love for each other (John 13:35). Jesus seeks our oneness with one another "so that the world may believe" that he indeed has been sent by his Father (17:21). The church's love and unity holds ultimate significance for the world as the visible basis of the gospel's power and legitimacy. In fact, the church is itself the promise of the gospel. The universal invitation to believe the gospel includes the invitation to enter the reign-of-God-produced community of the new humanity. Just as Jesus exhibited his union with his Father in obedient submission to God's rule and thus could say, "Whoever has seen me has seen the Father" (14:9), so too God has designed it so that when people have seen God's "peculiar" people, they have in a real sense caught a view of God. "As the Father has sent me, so I send you" (20:21).

---

30. Küng comments that while the church is a historical phenomenon, it is always more than it appears; this is what he calls the "invisible aspect" of the church (*Church*, pp. 59-65).

Representing the Reign of God as Its Servant

Jesus further believed it to be his mission to exhibit the signs of the presence of the reign of God by exercising its authority over brokenness, domination, oppression, and alienation. By virtue of his faithfulness, he was to be given a name and dominion above every other in the future. But even during his earthly ministry he demonstrated his authority over disease and nature, over people and their social structures, and over spirit forces that bind and distort. This authority must be carefully understood as an authority derived from being "under authority."

Perhaps the most interesting clue regarding the relationship between these first two facets of Jesus' mission comes from the most unlikely source. Luke reports how a centurion approached Jesus to request healing for his servant (7:1-10). He sent word to Jesus that Jesus need not come but only say the word, and his servant would be healed. He added, "For I also am a man set under authority, with soldiers under me; and I say to one, 'Go,' and he goes, and to another, 'Come,' and he comes, and to my slave, 'Do this,' and the slave does it." Jesus' immediate commendation of the centurion's faith affirms how the man understood authority — his own and that which Jesus possessed. One exercises authority only insofar as one is under authority. The source of Jesus' authority lay not in the powers he had as divine. His authority sprang from his own faithful trust and loyalty, his living under authority. In later chapters we shall see that there is a lesson here for contemporary Christian leadership who hunger for authority and power.

Jesus' healings, exorcisms, calming of storms, feeding of the multitudes, and raising the dead to life were all signs. These signs revealed that in Jesus' life under the authority of God the reign of God was at hand. The deeds themselves were simply doing what ought to be done under God's reign. They also point to what God intends the world to be like when God's reign comes. They represent what God fully intends to bring about at the world's consummation, when all that creation was envisioned and imagined to be is made finally true. The actions of Jesus show forth the horizon of the coming world of shalom — peace, justice, and joy in the Holy Spirit.

The church shares that horizon, and with it the impulse to respond to the whole range of need in humanity and in the creation. Thus the church represents the reign of God by its deeds as the servant to God's passion for the world's life. Like Jesus, it exhibits by numerous signs the reign of God, thereby exercising its authority.

To use Jesus' imagery, as the church is light to the world, so also it is salt. Going to all the earth, the church bears the mission to *do* all that Christ commanded just as it is to *teach* others to do the same (cf. Matt. 28:18-20). The fruits of repentance and the Holy Spirit's gifts of conversion bring about deeds arising from genuine discipleship. As we live under God's reign, our involvements with the world are repatterned.

The design for that repatterning is Jesus himself. Throughout his earthly ministry we sense the heartbeat of his action: compassionate response to human need. He was predisposed to be interrupted, even from his focal task of preaching, whenever hunger, sickness, demonic oppression, the grip of sin, social ostracism, or death crossed his path (Mark 1:35-45). Tears paved the road he traveled in order to bring good news. Such a predisposition was the theme of his keynote address in Nazareth (Luke 4:16-20) and the proof of his messianic appointment, as he indicated to John the Baptist (Matt. 11:1-6).

Far from being a distraction from his preaching in all the towns and villages, Jesus' compassionate responses to human need were an integral part of the message he preached. They were signposts raised to public view.

The church carries Jesus' mantle as the people of God "under authority." Our responses of compassion and service, like our actions for peace and justice, are deeds of authority and therefore signs that the reign of God is present now in our world and is on the way as its future. Our responses may be small and personal: a cup of cold water, a warm blanket, or a visit with cookies and cakes. They may be bold: "Rise up and walk," or the expulsion of evil spirits in the name of Jesus. They may engage the complexities of corporate modern living: pressuring governments and corporations for the sake of the disadvantaged or the ravaged earth, lobbying for just laws, solidarity with oppressed peoples, initiatives to cease hostilities among nations, care for marginalized peoples and the creation, or compassionate remolding of socioeconomic structures. Whatever our responses may be, they bring wholeness and dignity to the world and thereby provide a taste of a future in the reign of God under the rule and authority of Christ's lordship. These are signs that invite people to "enter and taste more, to eat and be full." They cultivate the hunger to pray the petition, Give us today the bread of tomorrow's heavenly feast. This eschatological rendering of the phrase from the Lord's Prayer is in keeping with the whole emphasis of the prayer as well as the meaning of the Greek text. When the church prays this way, the reign of God intrudes on the life of the world.

Representing the Reign of God as Its Messenger

Finally, Jesus believed it to be his mission to announce the presence of the reign of God and its implications and call. It was his mission to put into words what was true about his presence and his deeds. "Whoever has seen me has seen the Father" (John 14:9). "But if it is by the finger of God that I cast out the demons, then the kingdom of God has come to you" (Luke 11:20). Preaching and teaching with illuminating parable-puzzles and penetrating responses to situations in teachable moments were required to interpret what was seen and experienced. If his own presence was a *sign* of the reign of God, and his deeds were *signposts* pointing to it, his verbal proclamation of the meaning of his presence and deeds added the *signature*. Jesus is saying with his speech, "These things you see and hear mean that the reign of God has come among you. Receive it. Enter it."

The church shares this missional role as well. It identifies the reign of God by announcing its authority. The church's being and doing are irretrievably tied to its proclaiming. Its verbal interpretation of all that is lived and done makes clear where the real issues of life lie: "The reign of God is at hand!" The declaration of the message entrusted to the church gives substantial content and definition to what its being and doing signify. It affirms the character of what the world sees it being and experiences it doing. Jesus not only exhibited his oneness with the Father but also put it into words: "If you have seen me. . . ." He not only displayed the signs of the divine reign's presence, he labeled them: "If it is by the finger of God that I cast out demons. . . ." To proclaim the divine reign is to add the signature of Jesus; to refrain from proclamation leaves all else anonymous, ambiguous, and subject to misreading the situation. Such vocal signing makes explicit what is implicit in the other signs. Verbalizing the gospel of Jesus removes the ambiguity. It also renders the reign of God accessible. By it, the reign of God is opened to the participation of the whole world. Our words become the way to say of it all, "It's free! This community is open! You are welcome!"

Announcing the reign of God comes as a spontaneous expression of gratitude, humility, and joy when it occurs in the context of being the forgiven community that embodies the divine reign and signals its character in actions of compassion, justice, and peace. It is the simple response of the otherwise insignificant and lowly of the earth who have come into the freedom of a new identity in God's re-creation, an identity that was really true of humanity from the beginning. In proclamation we simply and profoundly name ourselves, and that is the place where ultimate power and authority lie. No repressive government, no oppressive social structure, none of the principalities and powers, not even death, can strip us of that power. "To all who received him, who believed in his name, he gave power to become children of God" (John 1:12). Our witness to the reign of God speaks in the voice of that God-granted right.

Proclamation is inevitable if our being and doing signify anything at all about the presence of God's reign. If in our being the church the world *sees* God's reign, and by our doing justice the world *tastes* its gracious effect, then the call to all on the earth to receive and acknowledge that reign begs to be expressed. That is why Jesus said it is necessary that his followers preach repentance and the forgiveness of sins in Christ's name to all the nations, so that all the nations may hear (Luke 24:47; cf. Rom. 10:14-17).

In summary, the church in mission may be characterized as the sign of Messiah's coming. Our being, doing, and speaking are signs that his coming is "already" and "not yet." He is here already or the signs would not be present. He is coming still or the signs would not be muted. Broken though they may be, the signs persist in the world by the Spirit's insistence, and they spell hope for the renewal of the human community in the final reconciliation of all things to God through the Lord Christ. In this respect, the church is the preview community, the foretaste and harbinger of the coming reign of God.

Further, it is important to hold these three facets of the church's mission together in synoptic vision, to look, as it were, through all three lenses at once in order to see mission whole. Synergy, not competition for primacy, exists among the three in the mission of the church. Wherever the Bible evidences a priority for one or another of these three aspects of representing the reign of God, we are quickly reminded how each implicates its two counterparts.

Finally, the three facets of mission illuminated by this vision directly answer the most fundamental questions and challenges for the contemporary church. They signal three basic priorities for the church's recovery of its missional soul.

First, in a free world of the autonomous and decentered self, and with a gospel of reconciliation in Christ, the churches must revive what it means to be communities of the reign of God. Churches are called to be bodies of people sent on a mission rather than the storefronts for vendors of religious services and goods in North American culture. We must surrender the self-conception of the church as a voluntary association of individuals and live by the recognition that we are a communal body of Christ's followers, mutually committed and responsible to one another and to the mission Jesus set us upon at his resurrection.

Second, in a secular world of privatized religious faith and with a gospel of Christ's reign over all things, the churches must discover what it means to act faithfully on behalf of the reign of God within the public life of their society. Because we live in a plural world that no longer gives us privileged place and power, we have the choice to confine our business to the private realm of the self and its leisure choices or to find new patterns for faithful public deeds. The calling to seek first the reign of God and God's justice means orienting our public deeds away from imposing our moral will onto the social fabric and toward giving tangible experience of the reign of God that intrudes as an alternative to the public principles and loyalties.

Third, in a plural world of relativized perspectives and loyalties, and with a gospel of the knowledge of God through the incarnate Christ, the churches must learn to speak in post-Christendom accents as confident yet humble messengers of the reign of God. A postmodern world is a wildly exciting arena for learning to speak boldly, often, and in fresh ways. The church speaks not to recruit members into an organization through an individualized version of the gospel, easily understood by an equally individualistic culture. It speaks boldly and often so that the signs of the reign of God in the Scriptures, in the world's history, and in the present may be clearly seen. It speaks so that the signposts to the reign of God evidenced in the church's own deeds will not be misunderstood.

The calling of the church to be missional — to be a sent community — leads the church to step beyond the given cultural forms that carry dubious assumptions about what the church is, what its public role should be, and what its voice should sound like. Testing and revising our assumptions and practices against a vision of the reign of God promises the deep renewal of the missional soul of the church that we need. By daily receiving and entering the reign of God, through corporate praying for its coming and longing for its appearance, and in public living under its mantle, this missional character of the church will be nourished and revived.

Truly and True

2002

I do not claim to be a scholar of postmodernism. But it is impossible to work at the missiological task of the church in the latter part of the twenti-eth century or the early part of the twenty-first without engaging the visions and sensibilities of what is variously called postmodernity, the postmod-ern condition, or the postmodern transition. While Bishop Newbigin did not often speak directly of postmodernism or postmodernity, his last great project to invite a missionary encounter of the gospel with modern West-ern culture stood upon the ground of the emerging postmodern critique of the most fundamental confidences of the modern age. The perspective of cross-cultural missionary experience that he brought to the encounter only strengthened the postmodern texture of his vision.

What I do understand about postmodernity has been helped along by numerous colleagues who themselves have studied its philosophi-cal assumptions and social characteristics at some depth. Many of these are colleagues in the Gospel and Our Culture Network in North Amer-ica with whom I have worked to fashion a vision for the church in a post-Christendom as well as postmodern world. For many of us the encounter of the gospel with Western culture precipitates the question of the church as a central challenge, even in North America where churches seem to be doing so well. Whatever surface successes remain, the truth is that beneath that surface lies a severe crisis of meaning and identity. There is a churning quest for a rationale for being church, and a hunger for the experience of being the kind of church for which there is a compelling reason.

The themes of postmodern transition and ecclesial identity come together in a newly emerging movement among younger "Generation X" pastors and church leaders in the USA and Canada. This generation knows itself to be a generation formed within the postmodern condition, or as they prefer to call it, the postmodern transition.[1] They recognize more intuitively than the rest of us that "postmodern" designates a movement away from something and toward something else not yet present or identifiable. This is an on-the-way place for the culture, not an assured ending place. They know this to be liminal time.[2] In the midst of it, they have a keen sense that ministry and evangelism in this time involve a dialogue among church, gospel, and culture, a dialogue unlike any that has gone before. They have not been willing to accept the forms of church inherited from the Christendom- or Enlightenment-shaped world, not even the so-called contemporary or seeker-oriented church of the baby boomers which embodies the values of modernity that are now passing. This rising generation of leaders poses instead some fundamental questions about the nature of community and truth and mission. Their experience of Christian faith within the postmodern transition suggests that a contextual, missional ecclesiology must be at the center of the agenda for us all.

It is in light of these quests for knowing the meaning and vitality of the church that I have chosen to address "the church in the postmodern transition." This means that I am not so much looking at "Enlightenment, Modernity, and Postmodernity" from a historical or analytical point of view. Rather, I am addressing what I take to be a fundamental missiological challenge at the present time in view of that sociocultural heritage. By taking up the issue of an ecclesiology for such a setting, I hope to address some of the who, why, where, and how questions regarding the church's calling to be the sent people of God. I would like to do this by identifying three dynamics which I believe are made crucial for the church in light of the current moment, given what we inherit from the shaping forces of Enlightenment and modernity in the past and what faces us in the emerging postmodern present and future.

1. Jimmy Long's book *Generating Hope* (Downers Grove, IL: InterVarsity, 1997) shows the correspondence between the literature on postmodernity and that on so-called Generation X. Bringing the two analyses together forms the basis for his helpful proposals for ministry among a postmodern generation.

2. See Alan J. Roxburgh, *Missionary Congregations, Leadership, and Liminality* (Harrisburg, PA: Trinity Press International, 1997), for the use of liminality as a lens for interpreting the current cultural situation.

Truly the Community

I take the phrase from the title of one of Marva Dawn's books.[3] By it I mean to say that somehow the forms of church we have inherited have construed church in a very different way from being a community, and the recovery of being community is fundamental for the church at the present time. The newly arising generation certainly will not tolerate anything less. More than that, it is what we discover in the Scriptures to be the crucial element in the Holy Spirit's presence in the world, to fashion the church as "a body of people sent on a mission" (to borrow a phrase from David Bosch in a 1991 lecture series).

Such a vision has been thwarted and muted under other conceptions of church which have shaped how we do things. The subtle notion that the church is "a place where certain things happen" has held increasing sway since the time of the Reformation. In the American context this has persisted, but under forces peculiar to the USA this shaping notion has taken an additional turn, an economic one. Essentially, two hundred years of history have seen the churches shaped more and more around a conception of what a church is that is shared by people in churches as well as outside them: the church is "a vendor of religious services and goods."[4] The grammar of everyday conversation illustrates how deeply this is ingrained. In a recent newspaper article about one church's decision regarding its historic facility and a proposed rebuilding project, there is an example: "For others associated with Graafschap Christian Reformed Church, a church must pay the price to keep up with the times and better serve its congregation." Something called "church" has the function of serving something called "its congregation." In this vendor model, members of the congregation are reduced to consumers of services, staff and leaders are the production managers and sales force, the goal becomes member (a.k.a. customer) recruitment, and

---

3. Marva J. Dawn, *Truly the Community: Romans 12 and How to Be the Church* (Grand Rapids: Eerdmans, 1992). The original title, *The Hilarity of Community: Romans 12 and How to Be the Church,* was changed to the current title in 1997.

4. For a more complete survey of the way this has emerged and the consequences of it, see George R. Hunsberger, "Sizing Up the Shape of the Church," in *The Church between Gospel and Culture,* ed. George R. Hunsberger and Craig Van Gelder (Grand Rapids: Eerdmans, 1996), pp. 333-46, and Darrell L. Guder, ed., *Missional Church: A Vision for the Sending of the Church in North America* (Grand Rapids: Eerdmans, 1998), especially chap. 4. See also Philip D. Kenneson and James L. Street, *Selling Out the Church: The Dangers of Church Marketing* (Nashville: Abingdon, 1997).

the gospel becomes a commodity needing to be appropriately packaged and marketed. The relationship between a church and its members is shaped around a pattern of vendor-consumer, provider-client relationships.

Here, I believe, is where we have inherited some of the harshest consequences of the Enlightenment. Critics of post-Enlightenment modernity, including Newbigin, have noted many of its features that beg for the gospel's missionary encounter: its confidence in autonomous human reason, its belief in the individual as the unit of identity and survival, its dichotomy between public facts and private opinions, and its reliance on effect and progress as the validation of what is right and true. But in modernity it is also the case that the rationalization of social systems and the process of routinization within social institutions have had a profound effect on the forms of church we inherit, and this needs as radical an engagement. Recent sociological interpretation of the history of churches in America suggests that the same rational choice theory which explains economics explains also the experience of churches.[5] As has been the case in other arenas as well, the economic part of life has come to define a whole range of institutions and organizations, not merely the commercial ones. The church is among them.

So the question is, What is the church? Is it an entity that exists for its members, to nurture their faith and give opportunities for their service? Or is it the members themselves who exist for the purposes God has in mind for them? Between the two views there lies a deep gulf. At present it is the first that defines the church and sets in motion its patterns of language and practice. But the church's birthright, possessed by all the people of God, is that it is a divinely called and sent community.

Several aspects of a reemerging vision for being truly the community have begun to take shape.[6] First, to be community means to possess a collective discipleship. The normal habit of speech, teaching, preaching, and even group Bible discussion is to emphasize the way biblical texts challenge and nourish growth in each individual's relationship with God and response to the gospel. In contrast to this the church is called into being to be a discerning community which receives the scriptural text as addressed to it corporately, which seeks the mind of the Spirit for its corporate calling

5. For a defense of this line of interpretation, see Roger Finke and Rodney Stark, *The Churching of America, 1776-1990: Winners and Losers in Our Religious Economy* (New Brunswick, NJ: Rutgers University Press, 1992).

6. The following three aspects of community, along with several others, are more fully developed in George R. Hunsberger, "Features of the Missional Church: Some Directions and Pathways," *Reformed Review* 52, no. 1 (Autumn 1998): 5-13.

and mission, which moves as one body in its expression of the gospel. The church is not a mere collectivity of individual disciples but together is a follower of Christ, in whose calling each one participates. The individual is not lost, but rather found, in its bondedness within the community.

Second, to be community means to gather for worship together. As a friend of mine has put it, worship has become a substitute for the church. Worship is something one goes to, something provided by professional staff. To be community again will invert this pattern. The church is the community. Worship is something that community does.

This makes a difference in the character of worship. It has the quality of being gathered up out of the collective praise and adoration and confession and pleading and hearing and responding of the community. This will mean, of course, a shift from professional planning and production toward worship that is the fruit of the work *(leitourgia)* of the laity to give expression to their praise. Persons of the community gifted for the kind of leadership that sees, values, empowers, and puts to voice the praise of the whole people will guide the shape and expression of the worship moments in the community's life.

Third, to be community means to remain community while scattered. The question, Where is your church? requires a better answer than the geographic location of the facility. Where are the people who are that community? Where are they working, living, playing? Essential to a notion of community is a new recognition that the missional placement of a congregation lies precisely within the workplaces and multiple social worlds the people inhabit day to day. And with that comes a new appreciation that when separated to all those daily worlds, the community is still a community, bound the same way to each other and responsible together to be a community that gives expression to the gospel. The church that is truly the community will be one in which there is a seamless harmony between its gathered moments and its scattered ones.

It is obvious that the portrait of community given here requires a serious and sustained critique of clericalism and a reversal of its manifestations in the life of churches that are now essentially "owned" by the clergy. Bishop Newbigin himself flagged this issue as one of the most crucial for the church living beyond Christendom, but this has tended to be missed by most of his readers.[7] New images and practices of leadership will have to

7. Lesslie Newbigin, *Foolishness to the Greeks: The Gospel and Western Culture* (Grand Rapids: Eerdmans, 1986), pp. 141ff.

emerge in which leaders find the formation and discipling of the community to be the first priority. What is needed is leadership that is an extension of the community, not a displacement of it.

Community of the True

If this rising generation is one hungry for connection, as so many have observed, it is also eager to find meaning. The acid test for people who claim to offer it is authenticity. It is not enough for the church merely to be community for people, hungry as they may be for even the most minimal sort of human connection. As David Lowes Watson has observed, the intimacy experienced in the small-group movement has the potential to be a mere "spiritual amphetamine," producing an immediate high but offering no sustaining life.[8] His own efforts to cultivate Covenant Discipleship Groups on the pattern of John Wesley's class meetings strike the necessary chord: "Christian Formation through Mutual Accountability."[9] The challenge is to be a community that bears the shape of the gospel, that is molded by the Spirit to represent distinctly the regime of God. The vision is to be genuinely Christian community.

I express that with the language of truth, but prefer to speak of being a community of the "true," a community that is "true to the truth." To say it this way is to stress that it is not a matter of holding the truth as a body of ideas, espoused, affirmed, and defended. But it is to embody a pattern of thoughts, language, and practices that is true to the truth that is Jesus the Christ.

I am using the term "true" here in the same sense that a carpenter might use it about the wall of a building when measured against a plumb line to determine whether it is vertically true. To say that a wall is vertical does not mean that the wall is the standard for being vertical. Rather it means that it corresponds to that standard which its builder has intended it to reflect.

There are distinct ecclesiological and missiological reasons for speaking in this way. It is a more modest way of understanding Christian identity

8. David Lowes Watson, *God Does Not Foreclose: The Universal Promise of Salvation* (Nashville: Abingdon, 1990), pp. 30-31.

9. David Lowes Watson, *Covenant Discipleship: Christian Formation through Mutual Accountability* (Nashville: Discipleship Resources, 1991).

to recognize that truth can never be so fully and rightly grasped that what is expressed is that truth. Not only the spirit of the postmodern age but the spirit of the cross-cultural missionary warns us to be humble about it. But having said that, it is still inescapable that Christian faith understands there to be truth, however inadequate is our way of comprehending it. Christians do believe (to use a phrase from the television program *The X-Files*) that "the truth is out there." That is, much as we must come to agree with the postmodern critique of modernity's confidence in reason, and the postmodern assertion that there is no one rationally defensible version of the truth and that all our claims to know it and efforts to state it are particular and provisional, nevertheless it is inherent in Christian faith that something is believed with "universal intent" and believed to have correspondence to some truth that actually is so.

This ultimate conviction of Christians is rooted in the incarnation. Wherever else *The X-Files'* search may take agents Mulder and Scully — investigating extraterrestrials, examining the paranormal, etc. — Christian faith is birthed by the presence among us at one time and place of one who embodied in himself the "truth that is out there." It is embodied and imbedded "in here" within the path of normal experience in an incarnation of the truth. He was the incarnation of the divine person. He said of himself, I am the truth.

The church knows that it does not embody the truth in the same way that Jesus is the truth. So while we do not claim for our creeds and actions that they are the truth, yet by embodying what is true to that truth, in all the particularity inherent in our doing so, we do claim that they correspond to the truth, which is the person Jesus. On that basis and against that standard, our creeds and actions are open to testing by all who observe and listen.

The recovery of the church's identity as community of the true rests on three perspectives about truth. First, truth is personal. If Jesus embodied it in his incarnation, truth is personal because he is that truth. In relationship and the revealing of a person to another it is known. Here is drawn into the picture the personal dimension of knowing which Michael Polanyi depicted and which Newbigin affirmed so often, owing in no small measure to the influence of John Oman in his theologically formative years. Oman had stressed the personhood of God, and Newbigin found that to provide a bedrock perspective for all his subsequent work.

Under the Enlightenment the West experienced a profound liberation of human reason. To speak of revelation does not deny the fruit the Enlightenment has produced nor that human reason is a source of the knowledge of truth. But it is to say that knowledge from human reason is always partial, and more than that, it is vulnerable to the bias and design of the interpreting human person or community. The postmodern hermeneutic of suspicion, which suspects all claims to knowing truth as expressions of a will to power, plays into this picture of things as a warning against confidence in the promise of human rationality.

Truth, if personal, is known in the relationship of persons. Here Newbigin's phrase about the revealing of God which comes to us in the form of Scriptures captures something important: the Bible is "that body of literature which — primarily but not only in narrative form — renders accessible to us the character and actions and purposes of God."[10] God as personal can and does act and choose the time and place of those actions, and those actions are that by which and in which God's character and purposes become known to other persons. In the end we are reminded that truth is then not some static, objective thing existing independently somewhere, but it is wrapped up in a willing, acting divine person.

Second, truth is perspectival. This is different from acknowledging that our knowing is always partial, or tainted. It surely is both. But to say that truth is perspectival is to affirm that it is inherent in the circumstances of life, created as they are by the one who is the truth, that human existence is by nature particular, contextual, and relational, and all knowing is relative to the language and culture creations that human societies establish, adapt, and transmit. Perhaps the point Newbigin made in *Foolishness to the Greeks* puts it most emphatically: "Neither at the beginning, nor at any subsequent time, is there or can there be a gospel that is not embodied in a culturally conditioned form of words. The idea that one can or could at any time separate out by some process of distillation a pure gospel unadulterated by any cultural accretions is an illusion."[11]

Here it is the vantage point of those who have experienced the missionary encounters of the gospel with the world of diverse human cultures that has companionship with postmodern sensibilities. Claims to truth beyond the particularities that shape all human life are relativized in both views. But in neither is there a necessary absolute relativity (which would be a contradiction in terms, at any rate). Rather, the relativity of knowing forces a communal and dialogical approach to all truth seeking. For the church as community of the true, that means at least two things: being true

10. Newbigin, *Foolishness to the Greeks*, p. 59.
11. Newbigin, *Foolishness to the Greeks*, p. 4.

happens in mutual accountability between communities of the true, and being true happens in the conversation with persons beyond the Christian community at the frontiers where Jesus as the truth is becoming known.

Third, truth is practiced. To objectify truth is to distance oneself or one's community from personal responsibility. Truth not lived, meaning that it is not believed with the will, can hardly claim to be truth. Philip Kenneson makes this point well in his essay entitled "There's No Such Thing as Objective Truth, and It's a Good Thing, Too!"[12] The church's vision of truth must mean that the verbs "believe" and "obey" become synonyms once again, as they were for the writer to the Hebrews and for Jesus himself. Only a practiced truth bears the stamp of authenticity and livability. In the postmodern transition, people do not look for better (objective!) arguments about God's presence or purposes, but they look for demonstrations of it being lived in terms of contemporary life.

In Missional Relationship

The church is not merely a community, nor is it enough for it to be a distinctly Christian community whose life and character increasingly correspond to the truth. It is a sent community. Its very presence as a distinct community is part of that for which it is sent, so even its attentiveness to being truly the community and the community of the true begins to fulfill its missional character. But it is called and sent to be present within the flow of the world's life, and in its life, deeds, and words to represent there the regime of the goodness of God.

Newbigin's conception of mission and of the church as missionary by nature takes on graphic form in his phrase "the congregation as the hermeneutic of the gospel."[13] Here he illustrates that the church is not merely an agency of volunteers for certain tasks of mission. Rather, its very being is the lens through which people view and comprehend the gospel. For the church, this raises the importance of the challenges of community and truth already mentioned. And it means for any particular church that the ongoing dialogue between the gospel and the culture of which it is a part

12. Philip D. Kenneson, "There's No Such Thing as Objective Truth, and It's a Good Thing, Too!" in *Christian Apologetics in the Postmodern World,* ed. Timothy R. Phillips and Dennis Okholm (Downers Grove, IL: InterVarsity, 1995).

13. Lesslie Newbigin, *The Gospel in a Pluralist Society* (Grand Rapids: Eerdmans, 1989), pp. 222-33.

goes on most deeply and sharply precisely within that church. This inward dialogue between the gospel and the community's culture, Newbigin would frequently say, is logically prior to the outward one in which the church is engaged with its world.

But outward it does and must become, and apart from that its own inward dialogue will be impossible. The church which is the fruit of the conversion encounter of the gospel with its particular culture is made by that encounter to be the demonstration of the life the gospel offers and the conversion it challenges. Out of that wellspring of its transformed life come its deeds in response to the vision of justice and peace which the gospel announces to be the intention of God for the world. Out of it comes also the clear and joyous announcement of the knowledge of God found in the person of Jesus the Christ. This holistic mission of life, deed, and word comprises the identity — the missional identity — of the church today. The post-Christian age awaits such a visible demonstration, tangible expression, and clear articulation of the gospel.

When talking about the way the church's calling sends it to re-present the reign of God, the eschatological dimension of it cannot be far away. The sent community is in a very real sense a precedent community, one which shows the intrusion of God's future. The missionary and eschatological qualities of the church have always been closely joined in Newbigin's thought. This was in evidence in his early, but still fresh, portrait of the church in *The Household of God.*[14] The church in this precedent sense is the foretaste community, a harbinger of the coming springtime, a herald of what is on the way.

The missionary and eschatological way of the church will need to be relearned. The long history of Christendom, including the recent phases of it as the functional reality in societies for which the legal forms have ceased, taught us to think in other terms. Now, without props from the social order and without a set role to play as its chaplain, whole new possibilities open up for the reemergence of the Western church's missionary identity.

But there are many potential pitfalls, most of all the multiple forms of the temptation to seize again some way of being for the society its orienting vision, to regain in subtle ways the lost position that so long gave the church large measures of power and privilege. It is here that I question the wisdom or appropriateness of speaking, as Newbigin tended to do in his

14. Lesslie Newbigin, *The Household of God* (New York: Friendship, 1954). See chap. 5, "Christ in You, the Hope of Glory," and chap. 6, "Unto All the Nations."

later years, about the way "the gospel as public truth" might be envisioned to have bearing on the forms of contemporary secular societies. The phrase itself, it seems to me, has several potential points of reference in light of the whole of Newbigin's work. If by "the gospel as public truth" he means that the gospel is fundamentally a news report, an announcement of the public events of God's actions as they have their center in the life, death, and resurrection of Jesus, and if he means to assert that those events are decidedly world news bearing significance for the whole of the world's life and are thus not to be relegated to the religion page, then his assertions must be taken with seriousness regarding the forms of Christian life and community and witness such a news report implicates. Such a report is to be embodied and portrayed in the public life of the Christian community, and testimony to it given in affirmation and critique among the powers of the world. In these respects the phrase is an important one, and one which has continuity with major themes throughout Newbigin's writings.

But if he means by it that the Christian vision is to be commended as a proposed basis for the unity and coherence of today's secular society, as the vision which alone is capable of giving the grounds for proper tolerance of all religions and a foundation for relating together the plural peoples of the society, then it seems to me that this moves once again in the direction of a certain kind of Christendom arrangement, albeit in a new form. On those occasions when Newbigin in fact made just this sort of move (and I can think of three such occasions in the USA in the 1990s when I myself was present), there were fundamental questions not answered. On what basis might, or could, the Christian vision be embraced or adopted by today's secular, pluralist Western societies? For a variety of reasons, Christians might want that or seek it, and might believe that it would be in the best interest of the society to do so. But why, on its principles, would or could the society choose to take the Christian vision as the basis for its unity and coherence? Unless, of course, it came to be converted to Christ, who is the center of the vision, in vast numbers!

To imagine that is to show the problem with the proposal. It suggests that a society might embrace the Christian vision as its basis quite apart from adherence to and allegiance toward Jesus the Christ. To imagine such a thing would be nonsensical, from the point of view of today's Western societies as well as that of the Christian faith. This, it seems to me, was precisely the problem with Christendom in the end, that finally the society had the shell of the Christian faith's perspective and ethos while no longer holding its essential faith. To use Max Weber's image, the gate to the iron cage was then flung open and has been ripped from its hinges. There's no putting it back. The captives are loose, and they won't be coming back to rebuild the cage.

For the church to return in spirit or form to a kind of relationship with the wider society that is rooted in the memory or remnants of Christendom will be to forfeit the next stage of its calling. A missional relationship implies life as a "parallel" community.[15] Such a community is not allergic to being a community of affinity with its surrounding communities, sharing common aspirations and quests as a people. Neither is it allergic to being a community of distinction from its surrounding communities, marching to the beat of a drummer who sometimes says dance when there is despair, sometimes says mourn when there is glee, and sometimes says refuse when all others move toward the destruction of life and hope.

Conclusion

In this postmodern transition, I have suggested, these three features will be required of the church: that it be truly the community, that it be a community of the true, and that it live in missional relationship with the world where it lives. The Spirit, I believe, moves us to such a journey and goes with us on the Way.

15. This phrase was suggested by Mary Jo Leddy at a conference of the Gospel and Our Culture Network in North America in March 1996. The papers of the conference, including the one presented by Leddy, are published in *Confident Witness — Changing World*, ed. Craig Van Gelder (Grand Rapids: Eerdmans, 1999).

Announcing the Reign of God

1994

It has become all too common, when attempting to ground evangelism in the New Testament, to resort to what we have called the Great Commission. The commissioning words of Jesus, variously reported at the end of each of the Gospels (Matt. 28:16-20; Mark 16:15-18; Luke 24:45-49; John 20:21-23) and at the beginning of Acts (1:6-8), are taken to be straightforward instructions, sufficient in their clarity to provide a rationale for evangelizing, no matter what the circumstances may be in which the church finds itself. But the need for a rationale — and the kind of rationale needed — is always shaped by the church's location in the social and cultural currents of its time and place, and by its character and life within those currents.

At the present time in North America, we in the churches find ourselves in a place rapidly ceasing to be a "churched culture."[1] Living in a post-Christian and pluralist society has sent shock waves through the psyche of our churches, shaking loose our long-accustomed security in the heritage of Christendom. This has brought us to the point of exploring the terrain in search of an identity beyond that of being merely a "vendor of religious services" for that niche of the population that exercises the private option to seek such services. We are thrust into a search for a sense of our mission in this new time and for the meaning of being witnesses to Christ in it.

The preachments and rationales of the past that do not specifically engage these new circumstances can only fail us. The growing disjuncture between the supposed clarity of Great Commission instructions and the

1. Cf. the use of this phrase by Kennon L. Callahan in *Effective Church Leadership* (San Francisco: Harper & Row, 1990).

practical behavior of large numbers of church members should alert us to this. In our situation, the instructions turn into an ever-amplifying exhortation to complete the assigned task. But what follows are either soft and fuzzy responses, in which anything that can be construed as lending influence in the direction of Christ "counts," or programmed schemes for structuring us all into activities that, by their very doing, are envisioned to achieve the task.

All of this is not to suggest that the commissioning words of Jesus have no relevance. It is to say that we must come to them in a new way, questioning what lies behind our tendency to focus on them and our way of seeing them as a rationale for evangelism. In this connection, two major problems present themselves.

(1) The first problem has to do with the way we tend to use the Great Commission as a rationale for evangelism. We appeal to it within a structure of thought oriented toward command and obedience. It is assumed, when we attempt to provide a biblical foundation for evangelism, that this is simply a matter of finding direct commands enjoining us to evangelize. It is further assumed that once such commands are found, evangelism is simply a matter of obedience. The presence of a command is thought to supply sufficient motivation for evangelism, and settling the issue of motivation is taken to be an adequate rationale.

This fails to ask questions about what lies beneath the command. Why was the command given? Why is it proper that, in a world with such a variety of other religious loyalties, we are thus commanded? How does the command make sense for us in Western societies today against the historical backdrop of cultural and religious imperialism? How can it be understood in a day when individual autonomy in matters of belief is asserted as a fundamental right?

More important, there are biblical reasons why our assumptions about a command-and-obedience rationale for evangelism ought to be questioned. In the first place, as missionary theologian Lesslie Newbigin suggests in his reflections on Acts 1:8, Jesus' statement that "you shall be my witnesses" is not so much a command as it is a promise, a promise linked with that of the coming Spirit. Newbigin urges: "Please note that it is a promise, not a command. It is not: 'You must go and be witnesses'; it is 'The Holy Spirit will come, and you will be witnesses.' There is a vast difference between these two."[2] It may be true that Newbigin pushes the grammati-

2. Lesslie Newbigin, *Mission in Christ's Way* (Geneva: WCC, 1987), p. 16.

cal point beyond what is warranted. But it is equally true that he has only touched lightly on a point of fundamental significance. Jesus' "prophetic promise," as Darrell Guder calls it, locates the accent in the text: being witnesses is not our assignment; it is our identity. "When the Spirit comes to [the disciples] and gives them the gift of power, their very identity will be transformed into that of witnesses. As such, they will carry out the ministry of that witness throughout the world."[3]

That this is an important point is underscored by another of Newbigin's observations, this time on Paul:

> It is, is it not, a striking fact that in all his letters to the churches Paul never urges on them the duty of evangelism. He can rebuke, remind, exhort his readers about faithfulness to Christ in many matters. But he is never found exhorting them to be active in evangelism. . . . Mission, in other words, is gospel and not law; it is the overflow of a great gift, not the carrying of a great burden.[4]

Paul surely envisages that evangelism will continue to take place. He assumes it to be appropriate, given what the gospel is. But he never urges it as a duty. It may be added that neither in Paul's writings nor in any of the other New Testament documents outside the Gospels and the opening verses of Acts is there ever an appeal to Jesus' Great Commission. It might be argued that the reason for all this is that the churches at that time simply found themselves evangelizing spontaneously and therefore needed no exhortation in this regard. Even if this could be proved, which is doubtful, the question with which we are left is not, "How shall we motivate a contemporary church which does not evangelize spontaneously?" but, "Why is evangelizing not now happening as a matter of course?" In light of the twin promises of the Spirit's empowering and the transformation of our identity to be witnesses, the explanation must lie at a deeper level than can be answered by some strong reminder that a command to witness has been given. Something more fundamental to the integrity of the church is at stake.

Accordingly, the first problem with an approach oriented to command-and-obedience, aimed as it is at motivating evangelistic action by a sense of duty, is that this approach mitigates the sense that somehow evangelism ought to be a spontaneous expression, produced by the Spirit and born of

---

3. Darrell L. Guder, *Be My Witnesses* (Grand Rapids: Eerdmans, 1985), p. 32.
4. Newbigin, *Mission in Christ's Way*, p. 21.

the overflowing of what comes from knowing the good news. As Robert Henderson has put it, "When a person, or a congregation, understands and has experienced the joyous news of the kingdom of God, evangelization is natural and spontaneous. People cannot keep such news to themselves."[5] The use of command-and-obedience as a rationale for evangelism thwarts the expectation of spontaneity, which is born of promise, not requirement.

(2) The second major problem with our use of the Great Commission as the principal text for establishing our evangelistic mission is that its use for this purpose is a relatively recent development. Until the advent of the "modern missionary movement" and the important stimulus provided by William Carey in 1792, this text did not play this particular role. In fact, prior to Carey's reappropriation of the text, it had been interpreted in a way that did not urge explicit missionary obedience. The commission was understood to have been made to the first-century apostles, and they were believed to have accomplished it by going to all of the then-known world. Carey dared to challenge this notion in his tract entitled *An Enquiry into the Obligations of Christians to Use Means for the Conversion of the Heathen*. He argued that if the command to baptize and the promise of Christ's presence are still in force, then the commission to preach in all nations must also be binding.[6]

Although the modern missionary movement found support in a number of texts (David Bosch identifies Acts 16:9, Matthew 24:14, and John 10:10 as crucial ones), the chief text to which it appealed is Matthew 28:18-20. By the end of the nineteenth century, this became increasingly the case. Obedience to this final command of Jesus became "a kind of last line of defense" against challenges being made to the missionary cause.[7]

Bosch's major contribution in his magisterial work *Transforming Mission* is that he identifies the ways in which the church's understanding of its mission in various historical periods was shaped by the cultural currents of the period and place. He shows, for example, how John 3:16 is characteristic of the patristic understanding of mission, Luke 14:23 of the medieval Roman Catholic missionary efforts, and Romans 1:16-18 of the Protestant Reformation period.[8] In the case of the modern period, for which the Great

5. Robert T. Henderson, *Joy to the World: Spreading the Good News of the Kingdom* (Grand Rapids: Zondervan, 1991), p. 131.

6. Cf. Harry R. Boer, *Pentecost and Missions* (Grand Rapids: Eerdmans, 1961), pp. 16-18.

7. David J. Bosch, *Transforming Mission: Paradigm Shifts in Theology of Mission* (Maryknoll, NY: Orbis, 1991), pp. 340-41.

8. Bosch, *Transforming Mission*, p. 339.

Commission and the emphasis on obedience constituted the heart of the missionary paradigm, the major motifs in the church's thinking reflected the influence of the Enlightenment. The essential features of this influence include

> the undisputed primacy of reason, the separation between subject and object, the substitution of the cause-effect scheme for belief in purpose, the infatuation with progress, the unsolved tension between "fact" and "value," the confidence that every problem and puzzle can be solved, and the idea of the emancipated, autonomous individual.[9]

In summary, Bosch concludes that

> the entire Western missionary movement of the past three centuries emerged from the matrix of the Enlightenment. On the one hand, it spawned an attitude of tolerance to all people and a relativistic attitude toward belief of any kind: on the other, it gave birth to Western superiority feelings and prejudice.[10]

Newbigin points out that the difficulty with post-Enlightenment use of the Great Commission was that it "could seem to validate a sort of triumphalist style of mission that accorded all too easily with the political and economic expansion of the European powers during this period, an expansion with which missions were (inevitably) so much connected."[11] An easy identification of missionary endeavor with the pride of enlightenment and progress lacks the critical principle for differentiating evangelism from an activity that merely underwrites the reigning values of the North American ethos. It fails to shape an evangelism capable of distinctive witness in a pluralist environment.

At a time when the church in North America finds that its social role has changed and that it is no longer the guardian of spirit and morality for the democratic experiment and that its faith is no longer the privileged option for understanding ultimate meanings and loyalties, it is essential that it acquire a new sense of what it is to evangelize. We in the church will need a new sense of missional identity that is more than the achievement of a man-

9. Bosch, *Transforming Mission,* p. 342.
10. Bosch, *Transforming Mission,* p. 344.
11. Newbigin, *Mission in Christ's Way,* p. 32.

dated task. And we need to develop a missional lifestyle that does not aim at conquest and cultural dominance. Any proposed biblical grounding for evangelism must address these concerns if it is to have force and relevance.

In light of the problems attending our traditional way of interpreting Great Commission texts, we may imagine that it would be easiest simply to dismiss them and to look elsewhere for biblical grounding. But, in the end, they must be dealt with, no matter where we begin. It is better to explore whether they may be reappropriated in a way that is both truer to their original function and more useful to our present needs.

To explore the function of the Great Commission texts in the New Testament is the place to begin. Before any of these texts had been written, the earliest church was already accustomed to sharing the "good news" with people in its social world. Certainly, this custom was not disconnected from the memory of Jesus' words, but it is far from certain that Jesus' words functioned as a command. Could it be that Jesus' words were intended for a different pastoral purpose?

Harry Boer concludes from his study of the early church's evangelizing behavior, as depicted in the New Testament, that "there is no evidence that consciousness of the Great Commission constituted an element in their motivation. . . . [T]here is no ground to believe that awareness of the Great Commission played a role in launching the Church on her missionary labors."[12]

Boer does not go far enough.[13] We must ask: If these texts did not launch the church on its missionary labors and did not provide it with conscious motivation, then what role did they play when they appeared in the Gospels and in Acts at the time they did? The central proposal of this essay is that we answer that question this way: *In the reporting of Jesus' final words in the Gospels and Acts we should see not a command for the early churches to obey but an affirmation of what they found themselves doing.* These texts are "evangelizing warrant," not "Great Commission." They do not mandate obedience to a mission; they validate the experience of being engaged in mission. Evangelism is not here required but authorized.

The predictive tone in Luke's two accounts is instructive. We have al-

12. Boer, *Pentecost and Missions,* pp. 43-44.

13. Mortimer Arias, in his otherwise fine commentary on the varying forms of what he prefers to call the "last commission," appears also to have missed the importance of critiquing the structure of command-and-obedience assumed in words like "commission," "mandate," and "task." See Mortimer Arias and Alan Johnson, *The Great Commission: Biblical Models for Evangelism* (Nashville: Abingdon, 1992), pp. 11-16.

ready noted the promissory character of Acts 1:8. In Luke 24, the missional warrant comes as an anticipation of the fulfillment of things long intended and already indicated in the Scriptures.

> Then he opened their minds to understand the Scriptures, and he said to them, "Thus it is written, that the Messiah is to suffer and to rise again from the dead on the third day, and that repentance and forgiveness of sins is to be proclaimed in his name to all nations, beginning from Jerusalem." (Luke 24:45-47)

Perceptions that, for the disciples, had been a long time coming are here expanded. The Synoptic Gospels share a structure that first shows how the disciples gradually came to grasp the fact that Jesus was the Messiah. Their confession to this effect marked the turning point at which Jesus "began to show his disciples that he must go to Jerusalem and undergo great suffering at the hands of the elders and chief priests and scribes, and be killed, and on the third day be raised" (Matt. 16:21; cf. Mark 8:31 and Luke 9:22). For the disciples to accept this seemed impossible, and even after the resurrection Jesus still helped them grasp this point (cf. Luke 24:25-27). Now, as Jesus underscores it again, something new is added. Once the disciples have understood that the Messiah must suffer and rise from the dead, they will need to learn where all this will lead: it is written that "repentance and forgiveness of sins is to be proclaimed in his name to all nations" (Luke 24:46-47).

This prediction will have been no easier for the disciples to grasp than the other points in Jesus' curriculum. It would be naïve to assume that the disciples immediately understood it and went out to fulfill it. Rather, this prediction stands as the unfinished story that precipitated for Luke the writing of his sequel, Acts. Luke begins Acts with a restatement of Jesus' prediction because he intended to show how the early church learned in stages what this meant. It learned the latter as the Spirit fashioned the disciples into witnesses to the risen Christ among all the nations. Acts was written, as was the concluding part of Luke's Gospel, as a way to remind the church later in its history of Jesus' earlier prediction. The church, from its later vantage point, could remember and understand. It had lived its way into it. The memory of Jesus' prediction affirmed and authorized what became true for the church. Whatever fears or second thoughts had emerged for it, whatever distance it might have felt as a second generation of witnesses, here was the warrant inherited from Jesus. This is the way things were meant by God to be.

If these texts in which we discover how Jesus envisioned and anticipated the future mission of the church are present in the Gospels and Acts
essentially as warrant and not command, then we may rightly search for,
and expect to find, texts in the rest of the New Testament that display the
ways in which such a sense of warrant took shape and root in the perceptions of the church and its leaders. We are not bound to look only for texts
that bolster a sense of evangelistic duty but are free to find whatever texts
respond to the questions that most press themselves on us in a pluralist
environment. Is our impulse to evangelize, to announce that the reign of
God is present and coming in Jesus Christ, legitimate? In a sea of opinions
and proposals about the meaning and direction of things, is it proper to tell
what we know about Jesus as though he is the power of creation and the
word of truth? In the face of such questions, a search for warrant opens a
new way for grounding evangelism in the whole fabric of the New Testament, not just in a few command-giving passages. It enables us to approach
biblical foundations from more than a motivational viewpoint and in full
view of our culture's critique. It allows us to explore what warrant exists for
the fact that, in the church, evangelism continues to "happen," that somehow the Holy Spirit is the instigator, and that evangelism takes place as the
overflow of the gospel among people captivated by the joy of the good news.

This way of exploring the New Testament needs more thorough treatment than I can provide here. But we can trace several themes so as to indicate the potential in such an approach. These themes show the kind of rationale for evangelism that lies implicit within the emerging mission of the
early church and is embedded within the warranting and predictive words
of Jesus prior to his ascension. Three themes will occupy our attention: the
evangelizing attitude present in the pulse of the gospel itself; the evangelists'
approach to people of a variety of cultures; and the modes of articulation
experienced and expected in the early churches.

(1) At the center of the message Jesus proclaimed was the announcement of the reign of God. This theme has been increasingly recovered in
recent reflections on the evangelizing mission of the church.[14] Still, as the
phrase comes into the casual parlance of the church, it picks up untested
assumptions about our relationship to God's reign. On the one hand, the

14. Three books that are most helpful in this regard are Henderson, *Joy to the World;*
Mortimer Arias, *Announcing the Reign of God: Evangelization and the Subversive Memory of
Jesus* (Philadelphia: Fortress, 1984); and William J. Abraham, *The Logic of Evangelism* (Grand
Rapids: Eerdmans, 1989). See also Monica Hill, ed., *Entering the Kingdom: A Fresh Look at
Conversion* (Kent, UK: MARC Europe, 1984).

reign of God becomes something we "extend." Especially among those with evangelical agendas, we imagine ourselves as those responsible to spread or expand the reign of God. On the other hand, those more concerned with the social implications of the gospel tend to speak about "building" the reign of God. Mission then has to do with establishing or fashioning the reign of God on earth.

There are problems with both assumptions. In the case of the first (to extend), the reign of God is conceived to be all "in here" and the church's mission is to be its CEOs, its sales promoters to extend it out to include more and more people. In the case of the second assumption (to build), the reign of God becomes a social project that we accomplish. It is conceived to be all "out there" awaiting construction by its architects, contractors, and carpenters.

It is noteworthy, however, that neither the expression "to extend" nor "to build" is ever used in the Bible to indicate the way we should see our responsibility regarding the reign of God. We find a parable about how the kingdom extends itself (Mark 4:30-32), but it is never said that we are to extend it. We find construction imagery having to do with the building of a congregation (1 Cor. 3:9-15), but the church is never equated with the reign of God, and we are never told to go out and build it.

What, then, are the appropriate verbs to use? In the Gospels, the most repeated and emphatic verbs directing our response to the reign of God are "to receive" and "to enter." They come, at times, intertwined: "Truly I say to you, whoever does not receive the kingdom of God like a child shall not enter it" (Luke 18:17). These verbs represent two image clusters that, taken together, provide a portrait of the identity of a Christian community and the stature of its mission. These clusters may be summarized as follows:

The reign of God may be said to be a gift we receive. It is something given (Luke 12:32). It is something that can be possessed (Luke 6:20; Matt. 5:9; Mark 10:14), but because it is yet coming, it is described as an inheritance to be possessed in the end (Matt. 5:5; 25:34; James 2:5; 1 Cor. 6:9-10; 15:50).

The reign of God may also be said to be a realm we enter. It meets us as God's welcome and invites us to come in. It is both a place to inhabit (Matt. 5:19; Col. 1:13) and a place yet coming that is to be inhabited (Matt. 7:21; 25:21, 23; 2 Peter 1:11). People can be "not far" from it (Mark 12:34). For some, it will be "very hard" to enter (Mark 10:23; Luke 18:24-25; Matt. 19:23-24). Some, in fact, "will not" enter at all (Matt. 5:20).

In a Christian consciousness shaped by these two images, there are serious dangers. On the one hand, there is the danger of presumption in so claiming to "possess" the reign of God that it becomes ours and not God's. On the other hand, there is the danger of pride in thinking ourselves to be securely "in." But it is by means of these very images that Jesus warns of these dangers: "I tell you, the kingdom of God will be taken away from you and given to a nation producing the fruits of it" (Matt. 21:43). "Truly, I say to you, the tax collectors and the harlots go into the kingdom of God before you" (Matt. 21:31).

It is in the dynamic present tense of these verbs "to receive" and "to enter" that there exists the greatest potential for a new way to conceive of our evangelism. The letter to the Hebrews uses the language instructively: "For we who have believed enter that rest. . . . Strive to enter that rest" (Heb. 4:3, 11). And again, "Therefore let us be grateful [since we are] receiving a kingdom that cannot be shaken" (Heb. 12:28). Here is a portrait of our conversion and its ongoing nature. We are those who, having been offered God's gift and God's welcome, daily receive and enter into the reign of God. This means that evangelism is construed in terms of companionship. We walk alongside others to whom the same gift is extended and to whom God offers the same welcome. We invite them to join us in the joy of daily receiving and entering into the reign of God. Evangelism, then, is not "to" or "at" people, it is "with" and "alongside" them. Evangelism as church growth or membership recruitment too easily serves our own personal or institutional interests. Evangelism consists rather in offering the gift of God and making welcome those whom God welcomes. The posture of invitation and initiation into a shared lifestyle then displaces the image of conquest and dominance. Evangelism in this posture is warranted by the nature of the gospel itself.[15]

(2) "If you wish to find the gospel, you must lose it." This loose and twisted version of Jesus' words may in fact provide the essential clue for understanding the struggle through which the church passed in its early years. At every point, the urging of the Spirit and the divinely appointed

---

15. William Abraham has caught the heart of this approach in his book *The Logic of Evangelism*. He describes evangelism "as that set of intentional activities which is governed by the goal of initiating people into the kingdom of God for the first time" (p. 95), conceiving conversion as entry into the kingdom. Because he has seen the "enter" side but not the "receive" side, his approach may too easily identify entering the kingdom with entering the church. To keep both verbs in view would provide a corrective. For a fresh invitational approach, see Raymond Fung, *The Isaiah Vision: An Ecumenical Strategy for Congregational Evangelism* (Geneva: WCC, 1992).

occasion of the moment pushed the church into an evangelizing beyond its understanding and challenged its assumptions about appropriate forms of belief, conversion, and worship. The first encounter for a church was with cosmopolitan Jews at Pentecost and then with Samaritans in the surrounding area. The conversions of an Ethiopian traveler, a god-fearing Roman soldier, and a diverse Gentile community in Antioch brought increasing pressure to bear on a church trying to figure out what it meant for people of a diversity of cultures to become captivated by the risen Lord. Jesus was very Jewish, but the mission into which the church had been thrust began to burst the wineskins to which these Jewish Christians were accustomed. Gradually, they became convinced that this was in fact what made their mission so universal and compelling.

Paul was the figure pushed to the front of these developments. His own sense of freedom from the law led him to the affirmation: "There is no longer Jew or Greek, there is no longer slave or free, there is no longer male or female; for all of you are one in Christ Jesus" (Gal. 3:28). But in an important sense, Paul also believed a variation on that language: "In Christ there is both Jew and Greek, there is both slave and free, there is both male and female." That is to say, Paul's affirmation of the essential oneness across hues of race, culture, class, and gender depended upon his affirmation of the integrity of the varieties of culture and heritage. Paul fought for the rights of Gentiles not to be forced into a Jewish mold. His experience of the grace of God was that it always moved beyond the ways in which it had thus far been grasped and embodied.

Nowhere does Paul more clearly articulate his missionary approach than in 1 Corinthians 9:14-23. Here he affirms that we only find the gospel, we only participate in it, in our evangelism (v. 23). And evangelism consists in losing the gospel, giving it away. Paul counted it as his greatest reward to offer the gospel free of charge (v. 18). His greatest freedom in the gospel was to make himself a slave to all (v. 19). His greatest success for the gospel was found in becoming weak (v. 22). Paul's approach was in sharp contrast to the tendencies present in the Corinthian church at that time, tendencies not uncommon for the church in any time or place. The church there had impulses that cut the nerve of a missionary gospel and prevented them from being a missionary congregation. These people held the gospel in their grasp, in knowledge and strength. Their grip on the gospel was so tight that they refused to permit other responses to it or expressions of it. Others had to follow their particular leader (chaps. 1–3), exercise their spiritual gift (chaps. 12–14), and share their knowledge about meat offered to idols (chap. 8). At the height of contradiction, they required that others share their freedom! In other words, the Corinthians held a monopoly on the gospel. It had become domesticated in their hands.

Mission in such circumstances becomes religious egoism. Evangelism becomes recruitment. Paul's assertion that he offers the gospel free of charge draws the contrast. Is the gospel something required of people at the gate, or is it to be given away to people outside the gate? Are we to grab people to the gospel, or open up the gospel to them? Does the gospel bring people to us, or does it join us to other people?

Paul's own policy of identification with those among whom he offered the gospel free of charge opposes the tendency to restrict the gospel to a single cultural form. Of course, there is always the matter of the truth and integrity of the gospel; but these Paul preserved, while exhibiting his freedom to be enslaved to other cultural forms and styles. To those under the law he became like one under the law (although he was sure that in certain senses he was no longer "under" it). To those without God's law, he lived as they did (although he knew that he lived under Christ's law and dared not violate that). Paul's cultural identification was not uncritical, but he refused the path of cultural domination and imposition. He was willing to give the gospel away to new possessors of it and to lose it to their new styles, responses, and definitions. There he expected to see it sparkle, startle, surprise, and shine.

Paul was not unaware that there is a certain weakness in this strategy. But it is this very weakness that most validates the evangelizing mission of the church. We can be no less vulnerable than were those who brought the gospel to us and released it into our hands, or no less vulnerable than God has been to offer the divine reign as a gift and a welcome. For us as for Paul, it is in the weakness of giving the gospel away and losing our grasp on it as its sole possessors that we participate in it most fully. As we see something in the response of another that reveals our own blind spots, we hear again its call to repentance. As we watch the gospel affirm acceptance to others with idiosyncrasies of their own, we know more deeply that we, too, share in the gospel's accepting grace. In other words, we become evangelized by those to whom we give the gospel.

To Paul's way of thinking, particularity is not alien to the missionary impulse. It is the path along which the gospel travels as each receives from another the witness of the Spirit.[16] The gospel, which is always expressed

---

16. It is one of the major contributions of Lesslie Newbigin that he has fashioned a theology of cultural plurality that sees in our election to be bearers of the blessing the critical

within the terms of some particular culture, is intended for the peoples of all the nations. A consciousness of these cultural dynamics and an approach to people that envisions giving the gospel away to them are crucial for a warranted form of evangelism in our current pluralist environment. Lamin Sanneh has put it well that "for all of us pluralism can be a rock of stumbling, but for God it is the cornerstone of the universal design."[17]

(3) In the New Testament literature, we observe Paul and we know that we see an evangelist at work. What he says about evangelizing is complemented by the ways we see him at work. We also catch the pulse of the work of the four "evangelists" in the written Gospels they have given us. The nature of the literature is such that these will be foremost as we explore the New Testament. Yet our perspectives will be skewed if we do not take note of the evangelists that did not write letters or Gospels. It is to the specific congregations that I refer. Clues about them may be fainter, but the substructure of living congregations bearing faith, love, and hope provides the foundational witness of the first-century church.

Especially intriguing is the portrait Paul gives of the newly formed community of believers at Thessalonica. Paul wrote 1 Thessalonians not many months after he first visited there and they first heard the gospel. Already, Paul affirms, they have proved to be imitators of him and his companions, who brought the gospel not only in word but in power, in the Holy Spirit, with full conviction, and with personal integrity (1 Thess. 1:5-6). In their willingness to believe openly, even against the pressure of direct persecution, the Thessalonians have already grown to be imitators of Jesus (1:6) and of the churches of God in Judea (2:14). In so short a time they have become examples of what believers are like (1:7); their faith — and the word of the Lord with it — has become known across their own province and the adjoining one (1:8). What has so profoundly demonstrated their faith is the

---

feature that unites particularity and universality. This is expounded most fully as the central theme of *The Open Secret* (Grand Rapids: Eerdmans, 1978 [rev. ed., 1995]). For an exposition of his view, see George R. Hunsberger, "The Missionary Significance of the Biblical Doctrine of Election as a Foundation for a Theology of Cultural Plurality in the Missiology of J. E. Lesslie Newbigin," PhD diss., Princeton Theological Seminary, 1987 [published as *Bearing the Witness of the Spirit* (Grand Rapids: Eerdmans, 1998)].

17. Lamin Sanneh, *Translating the Message: The Missionary Impact on Culture* (Maryknoll, NY: Orbis, 1989), p. 27. Other important books on evangelism that attempt to take pluralism seriously include Lesslie Newbigin, *The Gospel in a Pluralist Society* (Grand Rapids: Eerdmans, 1989), and Donald C. Posterski, *Reinventing Evangelism: New Strategies for Presenting Christ in Today's World* (Downers Grove, IL: InterVarsity, 1989).

visible change in their patterns of living: they have turned away from loyalty to idols, they serve a living and true God, and they live in hope, waiting for the risen Son of God to come from heaven at the time of justice (1:9-10). Of course, in the letter as a whole Paul matches these affirmations with encouragement to the Thessalonians to grow in these traits that already characterize them. All is not finished, but even at this embryonic point in the life of their church their evangelizing quality is most evident.

It will not do to drive a wedge between actions and words and claim that Paul only affirms the lifestyle of the Thessalonians as though that were somehow sufficient. What Paul affirms about them could not have been observed had they been a silent group. The new orientation of their lives and the hope they held must certainly have found expression in language and confession. Word and deed were bound together in the way the congregation demonstrated — in living, embodied form — what the gospel is.

Whatever else may be said about modes of articulation appropriate to the gospel's announcement, embodiment is the essential feature of them all. Paul always invited his hearers to test his words against what they experienced him to be (e.g., 1 Cor. 2:1-5; 2 Cor. 1:12; 4:1-3; 6:3-10; 1 Thess. 2:1-8). In 1 Peter, the encouragement given to the churches rests on the same foundation: "Always be ready to make a defense to anyone who demands from you an accounting for the hope that is in you" (3:15). The assumption is that the presence of such a hope is an observable thing, demonstrable to public view by the community that embodies the gospel.

We are talking here about something much more substantial than the emphasis in evangelism training circles several decades ago. Then, the emphasis was more on encouraging consistent moral behavior because, otherwise, the gospel would be invalidated by violations of the accepted norms of the society everyone assumed the gospel affirms. Now, however, when such a correspondence of values no longer exists and announcing and living the gospel proposes a very different, alternate style of believing and living, demonstrating the gospel in life is not merely for the sake of keeping the way clear for a hearing of the gospel. The demonstration itself shows what the gospel is about. The congregation is the "hermeneutic of the gospel," the only lens through which people see and interpret what the gospel is about and how it may be embraced.[18] Donald Posterski stresses this when he says that in our modern pluralist setting "the gospel will be perceived as a feasible alternate when those who do not know God have

---

18. Cf. Newbigin, *The Gospel in a Pluralist Society,* pp. 222-33.

some positive, personal experiences with people who do know him. Modern Christians have both the privilege of and the potential for becoming spiritual meaning-makers."[19]

A variety of modes of articulation of the gospel commend themselves as biblically warranted and contextually relevant today. One is the mode of the "witness," one who testifies on the witness stand in a trial and attests to what cannot be known in any other way.[20] Another is the "journalist," one who reports the public news that the reign of God is at hand.[21] Another model is that of "docent," in the sense of the way museums use docents. The evangelist as docent is one who interprets the meaning of what is experienced in the world. Finally, we may add the "rhetor," who makes the case that the gospel reveals the meaning of life and who urges the appropriate response. But it is required of all of these that they be grounded in an evangelistic commitment to a living embodiment of the gospel in tangible communities of faith, love, and hope.[22]

It is essential to the gospel that the gift of the reign of God and God's welcome to it not be withheld from but be genuinely offered to the world. It is essential to the church's mission that the gospel be given away to all to be embraced by them in their cultural particularity. And it is essential to the church's identity that it be a living embodiment of the gospel, demonstrating by word and deed what it means to believe and hope in the gospel. Taken together, these facets of the fabric of the New Testament link up with Jesus' warranting words to show how fundamentally valid and indispensable is the witnessing character and role of the church. The Spirit's persistent action to make the church such a witness is the confirming testimony.

---

19. Posterski, *Reinventing Evangelism*, p. 32.

20. Lesslie Newbigin, *The Light Has Come: An Exposition of the Fourth Gospel* (Grand Rapids: Eerdmans, 1982), p. 14.

21. David Lowes Watson, "The Church as Journalist: Evangelism in the Context of the Local Church in the United States," *International Review of Mission* 72 (January 1983): 57-74.

22. Darrell Guder's stress on an incarnational understanding of mission provides a valuable resource at this point. See his *Be My Witnesses*.

Sitting on Both Sides

1993

It strikes me as a curious, even bothersome, way of putting things to speak of the church's "mission to Western culture." The preposition "to" is the sticking point. If we are really talking here about culture (i.e. a commonly shared web of understandings of the way things are and a shared map for how life should be lived), then what would it mean to speak of a mission "to" a culture, whether our own or any other? Mission certainly reaches in the direction of the people of a society, those who together share a particular culture and both shape it and are shaped by it. And it has to do with addressing the powers that operate in the social arrangements and institutions of a particular people. But it does not so much direct itself "to" the shared culture of those people and powers as it happens always "within" that cultural framework. It addresses people and powers in such a way that it calls forth in them an encounter between the cultural understandings and values by which they live and the challenging impact of the gospel's announcements about the reign of God.

Once we understand this, we are warned against conceiving the "gospel and culture" encounter as one that is merely a matter of audience analysis, as though it has only to do with sizing up the thoughts, feelings, and values of the target population to make our communication of the gospel sharper. Nor is it adequate to conceive of the encounter as merely our effort to bring about changes in the personal and collective ethical choices of the society so that they more closely approximate the ideals we see to be those of the gospel. These responses, taken alone, too easily miss the more fundamental encounter that must engage the church if it is to be missionary, an encounter of the gospel with the inner, assumed logic by which the society orders its perceptions and actions. These responses represent the persistence of an "us to them" mission mentality too easily operating out of a conquering spirit or an urge to control, vestiges of a former Christendom that no longer lives anywhere but in the impulses of our minds. We were used to being a (or *the*) key force for shaping the social order. But whatever limited role we may earlier have had to influence and inspire the American social order has fast evaporated. With the shift in the church's social location in recent decades and the radical change in core values going on in the culture itself, we are faced with a crisis of mission identity and direction.

These factors have stimulated the emergence of the Gospel and Our Culture Network (GOCN) in North America. The GOCN is a collaborative effort that focuses on three things: (1) a cultural and social analysis of our North American setting; (2) theological reflection on the question, What is the gospel that addresses us in our setting? and (3) the renewal of the church and its missional identity in our setting. People from a wide spectrum of denominations and ministry vocations are working together in this network because of a commonly held belief that there is an integral relationship between these three — cultural analysis, theological reflection, and congregational mission — and that responses to the current pressures felt at any one point cannot be adequately engaged apart from the others. Those in the network do not pretend that they are the only ones addressing these issues. In fact, they are keenly aware that the ferment in each of the three areas is considerable and rapidly expanding. What makes this movement significant is the fact that it is drawn together by the central conviction that the current challenge and ferment is by its nature missiological and must be addressed as such.

What exactly does it mean to say that this set of issues is missiological in its essence? At the outset, a preliminary clue may be found in one particular critique of the Gospel and Our Culture movement as it first manifested itself in North America and in other Western societies. A major program of study involving missiologists from a wide range of Western nations was being headed by Wilbert Shenk under the title "A Missiology for Western Culture." In reaction to that phrase there came the challenge that it is inappropriate to call the Gospel and Western Culture project "missionary" precisely because it is focused on our own Western culture. This is because it was said to lack the one quality considered to be essential for defining what it means to be missiological: that it must be cross-cultural. For this critic, mission takes place in the crossing of cultural frontiers. Therefore, unless we are talking about moving across ethnic boundaries, mission in our inner cities, or something of the sort, we ought not to call the Gospel and Western Culture project missiological.

Undoubtedly, there is some fear here that, in the words of Stephen Neill's famous dictum, "If everything is mission, then nothing is mission." Or it may be feared that mission, the church's "sentness," will be lost in the church's self-absorbed attention to its own circumstances and the introspective retooling of its inner mechanisms. Such fears are healthy and warranted. But the required quality of being cross-cultural is precisely why our whole culture-theology-church agenda *is* missiological. By treating the full range of the current ferment as missiological, we are attempting to reinvest the North American church's identity and character with this cross-cultural quality, a dynamic that becomes emphatically present when we are engaged in the "missionary encounter of the gospel with our own Western culture" (as Lesslie Newbigin is in the habit of putting it).[1]

In other words, in this approach we are simply treating mission in our own cultural circumstances in the same way we treat the encounter in other places. There we enter as cross-cultural missionaries, and we naturally see the situation as a missional engagement. We also invite the fledgling churches that form in such places to encounter their own culture and to embody the gospel within it in such a way that its challenging relevance is felt. This we take to be their proper missional response. Surely, we assume, it is immediately their mission to do this!

We are only saying that now, for us who are in the place from which so many cross-cultural missionaries emanate, our most fundamental missional calling is to live the same way in our own culture that we counsel others to live in theirs. This we cannot do unless we are seriously attentive to the character of our culture, receptive to the shaping force of the gospel, and willing to bear our missional identity as a gospel-shaped community.

To state this point even more directly, being missionary and being a "sent" community — a "body of people sent on a mission"[2] — are not first about the church's outward-moving actions, whether actions to attempt to

1. Lesslie Newbigin, *Foolishness to the Greeks: The Gospel and Western Culture* (Grand Rapids: Eerdmans, 1986). See also two other books by Newbigin: *The Gospel in a Pluralist Society* (Grand Rapids: Eerdmans, 1989) and *Truth to Tell: The Gospel as Public Truth* (Grand Rapids: Eerdmans, 1991).

2. This phrase was used by David J. Bosch in lectures given at Western Theological Seminary in April 1991. The notion is fully developed as part of the "emerging ecumenical missionary paradigm" in his *Transforming Mission: Paradigm Shifts in Theology of Mission* (Maryknoll, NY: Orbis, 1991), pp. 368-89.

convert or actions to try to make a difference, whether actions close at hand or actions at a distance. It is first about how the church goes about those actions and the character of its own life in the process. This character develops not when a church — or its representative — leaves its geographic location. Rather, it happens when a church takes leave of cultural loyalties alien to the gospel. This step can and must lead to movement outward. But it must be the prior disposition if geographic leaving is to be genuinely missionary.

In other words, being missionary is about conversion as a way of life for the church, a way of life that shapes its movement to convert and its actions to make a difference. Our current movements to convert and make a difference generally do not arise from such a way of life. They are too much marked by a failure to recognize as intrinsic to our faith a fundamental departure (over against comfortable accommodations to the culture) and a sacrificial immersion (over against sectarian withdrawals from the society). As Donald Posterski has put it, we have ironically done what is seemingly impossible. We have inverted the dictum of Jesus: we are *of* the world but not *in* it. We have become "both captured and intimidated by the culture."[3] In our minds and hearts we have not sufficiently departed to the loyalties of the gospel, and with our hands and feet we have not become deeply enough immersed on behalf of the gospel.

The fundamental question before us in the churches of North America is this: Where is the church in the gospel and culture encounter? This question lies implicit in the phrase by which the movement mentioned earlier labels itself, a phrase borrowed from its companion British movement: "The Gospel and Our Culture." The power of the slogan lies in the little word "our" tucked in so innocently. At first blush it seems merely to designate which culture is being considered. That is, "it is not an Asian culture or an African one that is in view. This time around, it is the one we Americans and Europeans inhabit." But the word is much more significant than that. Its presence alters the mental furniture by expanding what we all too easily take to be a two-poled conversation (between the gospel and the culture) and forcing us to reckon with a third pole (the church). By doing that, the word brings to light and challenges a host of assumptions that ride with the two-poled version.

In the rich literature of missionary anthropology, we have grown accustomed to bipolar ways of putting the issue, and these undoubtedly push us to a shorthand way of talking about the current challenge as simply a

3. Donald C. Posterski, *Reinventing Evangelism: New Strategies for Presenting Christ in Today's World* (Downers Grove, IL: InterVarsity Press, 1989), p. 28.

"gospel and culture" agenda. H. Richard Niebuhr's watershed volume *Christ and Culture* set the pace for this. Sam Moffett, following Kenneth Scott Latourette, has tended to put it, "Christianity and Culture." Marvin Mayers follows suit in the title of his book *Christianity Confronts Culture*. Moffett and Mayers signal more explicitly what we and Niebuhr were really thinking all along. We somewhat automatically identified ourselves, those who are part of the Christian movement, as the "Christ" pole in the encounter. "Christ and culture" is taken to be about how we have related ourselves to the culture. More directly, the title of Louis Luzbetak's standard work, now revised, put the issue in terms of *The Church and Cultures*. In this title we have it more pointed still: the issue, as we tend to see it, is how the church relates to any and all cultures.[4]

Even in formulations that point in a slightly different direction, a similar identification of the church with the gospel pole tends to remain. The Willowbank Report shaped at the Lausanne movement's landmark Willowbank Consultation in the late 1970s used the rubric "Gospel and Culture."[5] The significance of that formulation was not directly articulated. It seems to help us move the discussion beyond church-centered assumptions to focus on the message from God. This is more emphatic still in Charles Kraft's reformulation of Niebuhr's categories. He compares various notions of the relationship between "God and Culture."[6] This is a more deliberate attempt to clarify the point that the issue lies beyond ourselves in the way that God, or God's message of good news, interacts with cultures.

4. H. Richard Niebuhr, *Christ and Culture* (New York: Harper & Row, 1951); Sam Moffett, "Christianity and Culture" (a course taught at Princeton Theological Seminary during the 1980s); Marvin K. Mayers, *Christianity Confronts Culture: A Strategy for Cross-Cultural Evangelism* (Grand Rapids: Zondervan, 1974); Louis J. Luzbetak, SVD, *The Church and Cultures: New Perspectives in Missionary Anthropology* (Maryknoll, NY: Orbis, 1988). One of Luzbetak's important contributions is his underscoring the point that not only do we have multiple possible forms of relationship to culture, but we actually relate to multiple cultures. The world of cultural plurality beyond Western civilization remained outside Niebuhr's purview.

5. The Willowbank Report, along with papers presented at the consultation, appears in John R. W. Stott and Robert Coote, eds., *Down to Earth: Studies in Christianity and Culture* (Grand Rapids: Eerdmans, 1980). It is interesting to note the way the ambiguity and identification of the church and the gospel are represented in the easy shift from the name of the consultation ("Gospel and Culture") to the subtitle of the compendium ("Christianity and Culture").

6. Charles H. Kraft, *Christianity in Culture: A Study in Dynamic Biblical Theologizing in Cross-Cultural Perspective* (Maryknoll, NY: Orbis, 1979), pp. 103-15.

But it is not so easy, even in such a formulation, to distance ourselves from identifying with that side of the equation (as may be evidenced even in the title of the book, in which Kraft poses his alternative, *Christianity in Culture*). Our role as the messengers, the missionaries, will immediately draw us back into the picture as the ones who sit comfortably on the gospel/ God side of things over against culture.

Increasingly, the bipolar way of speaking has given way to a sense that there are really three interacting poles: the gospel of God, the culture of a human society, and the community of Christian believers within that society. This triangular perspective is the model used by Robert Schreiter in his *Constructing Local Theologies* and Lesslie Newbigin in *The Open Secret*. Peter Schineller reflects a similar perspective in his book *A Handbook of Inculturation*. He describes the pastoral circle (a hermeneutical circle) as incorporating three poles: the situation, the Christian message, and the pastoral agent or minister. While it describes the dynamics involving a person facilitating inculturation, his model could as well describe the church's missiological role. Similar also is the way Carlos Mesters, in *Defenseless Flower*, describes the way the Base Ecclesial Communities read the Scriptures. He offers a three-cornered hermeneutical model of pretext (the life situation of the community), text (its historical-literary meaning), and context (the church's faith, what they "come with" to the text).[7]

The presence of the word "our" in the "Gospel and Our Culture" slogan indicates the same sort of tripolar conception, doing so in a way that underscores two important reasons why we cannot simply assume that we ourselves represent the gospel pole. First, our way of understanding God and putting the gospel can never be equated with the God who engages us and the message God addresses to us and the whole of the world. Our grasp and experience are necessarily partial; they are historically and culturally framed. We dare not treat this "gospel and culture" thing as though we fit easily on the gospel side of it. Second, we dare not assume that we sit at some comfortable critical distance from the culture part of the equation, that we somehow are placed over against it. We are never that distinct from our culture. We are participants in it. We are shaped by it, and it pervades our entire framework of meanings and motivations.

7. Robert J. Schreiter, *Constructing Local Theologies* (Maryknoll, NY: Orbis, 1985); Lesslie Newbigin, *The Open Secret: Sketches for a Missionary Theology* (Grand Rapids: Eerdmans, 1978); Peter Schineller, SJ, *A Handbook of Inculturation* (New York: Paulist Press, 1990), pp. 61-73; Carlos Mesters, *Defenseless Flower: A New Reading of the Bible* (Maryknoll, NY: Orbis, 1989), pp. 106-11.

It shapes in a particular way our capacities to hear and grasp and decide about the gospel that is coming to us from God, and it colors the form of all our responses to it.

We are forced by these circumstances to admit that we are not here dealing with a single dialogue. Rather, such a gospel-culture encounter always unfolds for the Christian community as a twofold dialogue: the dialogue the gospel of God has with us within our culture, and the dialogue we then have representing the gospel among the others who share our culture.

We are the community that has been grasped by the claim of the gospel, a gospel that has inaugurated us into a process of conversion by which the assumptions and dispositions we share with our culture are being challenged and repatterned along the lines of new loyalties, visions, and commitments. But we are aware that we are neither so fully and finally shaped by that gospel nor so unique and distinct from the culture as we may have wanted to think. We have observed this truth more vividly of late as we sense the malaise in our churches born of the loss of our former identity as the moral support and spiritual caregiver to the social order. We notice in our loss how little identity remains, how little we have been shaped by the force of the gospel. And we see how accommodated we have become to the contours of our culture. We have assumed too quickly that our initial conversions were enough. What we have failed to recognize is that the gospel's first-order encounter with the culture we inhabit will be with us, not with any "them" out there. The encounter is first of all an inner dialogue before it is an outer one; it is what Newbigin calls the internal dialogue, which must be antecedent to the external one that lies at the center of a missionary's proper concern. This is what is missing in George Hunter's admirable depiction of the "secular people" he is trying to help us know how to reach. The description he gives portrays our characteristics in the churches as well as it does those of our companions in the culture! The "reaching" must take place inside of us as much as out there beyond us.[8]

If, on the one hand, this inner dialogue with the gospel engages us, so the nature of our dialogue with those of the culture is reformed on the other hand. We do not approach the dialogue as though we are somehow outside the culture with its commitments and ways of seeing things. We join the dialogue as companions in it. But we recognize that the gospel has cap-

8. See Newbigin, *The Gospel in a Pluralist Society,* p. 56; George G. Hunter III, *How to Reach Secular People* (Nashville: Abingdon Press, 1992), pp. 41-54.

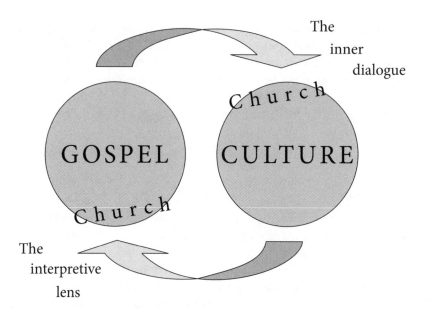

tured us for God in ways that have brought about fundamental shifts in our culture-given assumptions. And we know that this capturing has launched us on a lifelong path of being encountered by that gospel repeatedly regarding shifts still in progress. We expect the hardness and delight of encountering these shifts along the way. Our place, then, in the outer dialogue, born as it is out of this inner dialogue, is to be the God-given "hermeneutic of the gospel" (to use another of Newbigin's phrases).[9] We are present with them to provide the lens, the language by which they may grasp and be grasped by the same gospel. As a community, we display in numerous ways the announcement that God's reign has come through Jesus Christ. In particular, we make visible the way such an alternate view of things as is indicated by that announcement becomes a lived transformation within our culture's terms. We show that life can indeed be lived out this way in our culture's context. This dialogue with others in the culture, as the gospel's hermeneutic, moves us beyond truncated missiologies for "reaching" the culture. Mission cannot mean merely espousing a message or commending a belief. Nor can it mean merely claiming a divergent view. Rather, it must come to form as a lived, daily-life experience that demonstrates the healing the gospel produces.

9. Newbigin, *Gospel in a Pluralist Society,* 222-33.

These two dialogues are interlinked. Without the gospel's inner dialogue with the culture inside of us, there will not be an adequate hermeneutic for the broader society. Apart from the hermeneutical character of our dialogue with that society, we abstract the gospel and block its incarnation in us before watchful eyes. The church — the "us" of the "our culture" phrase — sits at the same time at both places in the gospel-culture encounter: we sit on the culture side, encountered there by the gospel that engages the culture first as an inner dialogue with us; and we sit on the gospel side, called to be the visible hermeneutic of the gospel in and for its encounter with the culture. To put it another way, in the gospel's encounter with our culture, the gospel meets the culture first here in us, in an inner dialogue; similarly, the culture meets the gospel first here in us who are the hermeneutical lens through which it may be perceived.

In this posture — sitting on both the culture side and gospel side — we must seek our identity. The crisis of the moment pushes us to it. The missionary essence of the church assumes it of us. The Spirit of Christ leads us there.

PLACE

Discerning Local Vocation

2004

When the Holy Ghost Full Gospel Baptist Church outgrew its facilities in one neighborhood of Detroit and moved to another, it assumed something not many churches assume. The move would mean that a lot of the members would now move into the new neighborhood. After all, they were going to be the community of God's people through whom God would show his presence there. Acquiring the grand old building that was once the Packard showroom placed them in a half-mile-square area along that stretch of Grand Boulevard that had once been housing for lower and middle management in the heyday of Detroit's automotive industry. Now, the housing had become run down, and the area was known for its drug dealing, alcohol consumption, absentee landlords, and downward economic spirals. Families were mostly broken ones. Despair had become the normal way of life for the people who lived there. But the people of Holy Ghost knew God well enough to know that the divine intent was to bring healing and deliverance to this neighborhood, and the fortunes that landed them in this facility were not accidental to that intent.

The founding pastor of Holy Ghost, Henry N. Lewis, had bred into the core of this church a simple, and often repeated, mantra: "Love everybody." If someone crosses your path, or crosses you on the path, "love everybody." If someone stumbles half-drunk into your church service, "love everybody." If violence is done to you by officials or un-officials,

---

This chapter was written on behalf of a team of colleagues seeking to discern in a number of congregations the "patterns in missional faithfulness" found there. For the full report, see *Treasure in Clay Jars*, by Lois Y. Barrett et al. (Grand Rapids: Eerdmans, 2004).

"love everybody." And when you plop yourselves down in a community by establishing your worship center there, your new neighbors are the obvious prime candidates for the same: "love everybody!"

From the moment the move was confirmed, the idea of "loving everybody" from a comfortable commute didn't seem to make much sense to the people of Holy Ghost. It was obvious: if not all of them, at least many would find homes in the new community and live alongside the "everybodies" God was sending them to "love." At least half the families of the church did that. While it was not their original intent, Pastor (now Bishop) Corletta Vaughn and her husband found themselves moving as well, from a more comfortable five-bedroom suburban home to the "Packard" community. (Hearing Bishop Vaughn tell the story of her husband's dream in the night that indicated God was calling them to move — an idea she wasn't ready to hear! — betrays the human realism of a woman who wanted and prized the comfort we all do, while it gives testament to her ultimate inclination to follow what God was indicating, comfortable or not.)

Shortly after the move, Valorie McCune was added to the pastoral team. She brought not only a gifted musical and worship presence but her concern for "Christian community development," a term John Perkins of Mississippi had used in workshops she had attended, and through which her vision had been galvanized. Perkins had become famous for his three Rs of Christian community development: relocation, reconciliation, and redistribution. The starting point was clear. She joined the others, including the circle of pastors and elders, and relocated herself into the neighborhood. If Holy Ghost Church was to be the healing presence of Christ in this neighborhood, anchored as it was in this new worship center now dubbed "the House of the Lord," it would be so as a community of new neighbors sharing life as other neighbors saw and experienced it.

Transfiguration Parish (Roman Catholic) in the Williamsburg area of Brooklyn had experienced a severe decline by the late 1950s. Originally a parish of German immigrants, the character of the community had changed. It was increasingly Puerto Rican immigrants who lived there, alongside a significant community of Hasidic Jews. When Father Bryan Karvelis arrived there, he knew that he was ill-prepared for ministry among poor Puerto Rican immigrants. His first instinct was to seek permission to live in an apartment among them. His own sense of vocation was formed by the spirituality of Charles de Foucauld, which focused on the mystery of the incarnation, how God entered the human condition and in fact took up residence among the poor of Israel. That vocation has passed, over many years, to the new congregation that formed and flourished in the parish. The large, vibrant Hispanic congregation of the present-day parish now bears those same marks of incarnation. Their reason for being is to be "present with Christ in the Eucharist and present with the poorest of the poor."

Central to Transfiguration's understanding of its vocation is the biblical understanding of the incarnation — God leaving behind power and glory (Phil. 2:5-11) to take the form of a peasant in a land of poverty. Pasqual Chico, a lay leader, talks with tears in his eyes of the wonder and awe he feels about a God who would lower himself in this way. It is this awe and wonder of the incarnation that draws parish "responsibles" (leaders of fraternities of fifteen to twenty people each) together on Saturday mornings for an extended quiet meditation, or eucharistic adoration, where the focus of worship is again and again the life-giving and life-saving sacrifice of Jesus Christ. When Pasqual and the other leaders, along with Father Bryan, emerge from the catacombs-like worship space beneath the sacristy, they share breakfast, discussing together the Gospel lesson for the next day's liturgy and the culture of our day that it confronts. Then they share lunch with a group of formerly homeless men who reside at the parish facility, some of whom comprise an unofficial religious order.

Members of our research team were welcomed to observe and participate in one of these weekly 7:00 a.m. to 1:00 p.m. Saturday vigils. They came away with a profound sense that this congregation seeks to *be* what it *believes*. Its vocation is to be the living incarnation of Jesus Christ — to be "present to God in the Eucharist and present to others — especially the poorest among us." Father Bryan says, "When you concentrate on being contemplative and with the poor, you really do change — your interests, your lifestyle are radically different." Pasqual adds, in a way that vividly captures this incarnational vocation, "We are Matthew 25."

The Vocation of the Congregation

"We are Matthew 25." "We have this ministry." "We have this treasure." "Clay jar though we are, the mercy shown to us is more than enough to set us on the path of bearing this treasure."[1] These are the attitudes that lie deepest at the root of what distinguishes congregations as missional. No grand program of success does it. No ambitious activism. No effort to change the world or win it

---

1. Cf. 2 Cor. 4:1-7.

back. Simply the humility of being God's servants. Being a missional church is all about a sense of identity, shared pervasively in a congregation that knows it is caught up into God's intent for the world. It comes from having heard, one way or another, the still, small voice that says, "You are mine. I have called you to me. I join you to my compassionate approach to the whole world for its healing. You are witnesses to what I have done and what I will yet do."

We are calling this "missional vocation." That is not a phrase any of the churches we visited would use. But it is what we discovered about each of them, that they are concerned to discern and follow their God-given vocation, their calling. They live at different places along the way. For some the discernment is a fresh quest. For others it simply happened to them as they tried to be faithful where they were planted. For some it's a very conscious thing. For others it's simply the way they do things. But for all of them there is a sense that they are here for some reason, and that reason is bound up with the call of God. They are in service to something bigger than themselves. The reign of God has captivated them in Jesus Christ, and increasingly it defines them. The mission of God defines what their own mission must be. Their mission is not defined by some discernable group of potential clients for whom they might provide certain services. Nor is it defined by identifying potential members of their organization, as though the task is one of recruitment. Rather, for these congregations it is a matter of faithfulness to a God-given vocation.

Vocation is a word that has gone out of fashion. When it is used, it normally refers simply to one's chosen career or line of work, one's profession, perhaps. In this regard, the meaning has slipped from earlier uses of the word, especially by Christians. For one thing, it conceives of vocation as a narrow band of activities — the work-related ones. Originally, when Christians spoke of their vocation, the word had greater depth and breadth. In his definition for the word, Paul Stevens picks up the fuller meaning of the conception. For him, vocation is "experiencing and living by a calling" in such a way that it "provides a fundamental orientation to everyday life."[2] *Calling* is the operative word here. In fact, the Latin root of our English word *vocation* is *vocatio*, which means "to call." All the ramifications of God's calling are in view: tasks, practices, attitudes, perspectives, beliefs, vows!

The other slippage is apparent when we so easily talk about vocation as *one's chosen career*. We may in fact refer to that as a "calling," but most often

2. R. Paul Stevens, "Calling/Vocation," in *The Dictionary of Christianity in Everyday Life*, ed. Robert Banks and R. Paul Stevens (Downers Grove, IL: InterVarsity, 1999), p. 97.

that is quite apart from a clear notion that there is a "caller." For the Christian, vocation has to do with being called by, and toward, someone! The call of God in Christ orients and governs the choices we make, which then become more like discernments of calling than they are personal preferences.

The book *Missional Church* was deliberate about describing the missional quality of the church as being "called and sent" by God.[3] These are not two separate acts of God, with one as the prior condition of the other, or one as the counterbalance to the other. They are one and the same! For the church to understand itself to be missional ("sent") is to discern its vocation ("calling"). To be called by God is to be taken into a way of life and mission. That is why Klaus Bockmuehl puts the issue this way:

> [Jesus] saw himself as a man with a mission, in the literal sense of someone who has been sent. Jesus' goal in life, his perspective, had been set for him. They were a divine commission and assignment. This is exactly what we call "vocation" in the life of a Christian. Our "vocation" is derived from, and the complement of, Christ's mission.[4]

But here we are speaking of vocation in a corporate sense, in reference to a congregation, and we believe it is right to do that. For one thing, there are biblical grounds for it. The Old Testament word for call *(qara)* is primarily used for "the people of God who are summoned to participate in God's grand purpose for the world." In similar fashion, in the New Testament the call *(kaleo, klesis)* is "the summons to holy corporate and personal living and the call to serve."[5]

This in no way denies each person's own vocation, each one's own calling, which will have its unique, particular contours. And of course, it is not hard to see that the collective vocations of the people of a congregation will have a certain cumulative effect on the character of the whole. But we are saying something more than that. The church as a whole, and each particular expression of it, is addressed by God in such a way that its vocation is "called" into being. When attentive to the voice of God, a congregation discerns not only that vocation that is shared across the whole church, but also its particular calling to express that vocation in its own place and time. This is discerned and followed together by a community. Its vocation is so

---

3. Darrell L. Guder, ed., *Missional Church: A Vision for the Sending of the Church in North America* (Grand Rapids: Eerdmans, 1998).

4. Klaus Bockmuehl, "Recovering Vocation Today," *Crux* 24, no. 3 (September 1988): 25.

5. Stevens, "Calling/Vocation," p. 99.

much more than the sum total of all the personal vocations that, in fact, it ends up being the other way around. *Personal* vocation is shaped and molded in the context of a community that has clarity about *its* vocation. A Christian's personal sense of vocation is a derivative from that "one hope of our calling" (Eph. 4:4) shared with the whole church, those "called out" *(ekklesia)* into the mission of God!

Speaking this way about a congregation's missional vocation should also make it clear that we are trying to reclaim words like "vocation" and "call" for the whole church. The words have tended to be used, almost exclusively at times, for the clergy or others in special offices or roles within the church. For Protestants, the question, Are you called to the ministry? conjures up very clearly an image that includes seminary training and ordination to an office such as Minister of Word and Sacrament. Likewise, in Roman Catholic usage, the word *vocation* is used mostly to indicate those entering religious life, especially the priesthood. Both are restrictive. Not only is it true of all Christians that they are called to ministry and therefore possess vocations, but it is also true that the church itself is called and has a vocation. Discerning it brings the church nearer to the heart of God, the caller.

The stories we tell are of congregations for whom it has been important to discern their vocation. And once known, to whatever degree of clarity, it has been their intent to pursue it and fulfill it. This has set them on a path that continually asks questions of location and identity. They have given attention to

- *where* they are, in a geographic, social, cultural context
- *when* they are, in the flow of history and change
- *who* they are, in continuity with a tradition, re-forming it in the present
- *why* they are, welcoming God's call, entering God's coming reign.

Following this path has required conversions of them, over and over again. But it has become the route of joy and hope for them because in their missional vocation is to be found their participation in the very life of God.

Local Responsibility — The "*Where* Are We?" Question

Holy Ghost's sense of responsibility is local, specific, geographic. If their missional assignment is clear socially and ethnically, it is because the geographic turf defines it that way. Its meeting place ("the House of the Lord"), and its residency, family by family, lie within a specific, poor, and socially rugged neighborhood, marked off by the boundaries of roads and ravines and political units. The move to that place, and thus that missionary territory, was a conscious one, prompted by the need to find a new facility. But at an important level, the church chose a facility and a neighborhood at the same time.

Transfiguration Parish, on the other hand, did not move its location 40 years ago when its present ethos began to form. Rather, the social character of the neighborhood had moved! The original immigrant population gave place to a newly arriving one, and everything was different from then on. The language went from German to Spanish. What continued were the dynamics of an immigrant population, but with a different experience of it by the new group. The economic realities meant the Puerto Rican population would have a tougher time catching hold of the ladder leading to prosperity.

In both cases, the neighborhood to which the church moved, or which moved toward the church, has had an impact on the character of the church's vocation, its sense of mission. Holy Ghost found its emphasis on "deliverance" would take on new meaning among people struggling with alcoholism, drug dealing, and family meltdown. Transfiguration was drawn to a spirituality that could sustain life together among the working poor, the street poor, and the poorest of the poor.

Eastbrook Church of Milwaukee represents another way that a sense of local responsibility came about. At its inception, the church made a deliberate choice. It was birthed in 1981 out of Elmbrook Church, a large and well-known church located in the western suburbs of Milwaukee. Its birthing represented a move not outward toward newer suburbs but in the opposite direction. A cluster of people, a number of whom lived more toward downtown, had come to share vision for a church *in* the city, and *for* the city. That early vision guided choices about the location of worship and ministry facilities, and it set the tone and character of the church. Ever since, the church's life has centered around involvement in the concerns of the city, relationships with other churches in the city, a focus of prayer upon the needs of the city, and a commitment to befriend city dwellers and welcome them to Christ.

Eastbrook's commitment to the city shows up perhaps most graphically in its clear sense of responsibility to serve city churches, regardless of denomination, by communicating personally and persistently with pastors and laypersons in order to pray for them and if possible to provide material assistance. Regularly, Eastbrook hosts worship and other activities that incorporate other churches' choirs and speakers with Eastbrook's. Two times a year, the congregation sets aside a week in which programs of ministry are set aside and the congregation gathers three times a day to pray. Each time, one of those days is focused on Milwaukee churches — their successes and their struggles. Prayer time each weekday at 6:00 a.m. throughout the year always attends to information about or from other congregations. Eastbrook sees other congregations in the region as partners, not as "them." They exist together for the city's sake.

For the West Yellowstone Presbyterian Church, the location of its responsibility comes from the character of their town. Wide swings of population, between a summer season filled with tourists and service industry workers and a winter season of year-round residents, make for an oscillating location for the church's missional vocation. The church has come to see itself as a church of and for the town part of the year and a welcoming community of worship for all for the summer visitors. They are stakeholders in both dynamics of the town's life. The character of the place has given shape to the church's vision.

Meanwhile, the IMPACT Churches of New Jersey have set upon an exciting but scary journey, taking them they know not where. Their current *raison d'être* is to ascertain what it means for them to be the people of God today, where they are. Is it possible, they are asking, for 300-year-old Dutch Reformed congregations to develop a sense of missional vocation for a new era in vastly changed and changing surroundings? It is in quest of missional identity — and some sense of the vocation it implicates — that these seven Reformed Church in America congregations in New Jersey have embarked on a journey together. And the taproots for the missional vocation they seek are the long history of their place, their long history in it, and the place and time to which those histories have brought them and their neighbors.

What can be said most about these IMPACT churches is that they are decidedly "in process" toward a missional *identity* (who we are), missional *engagement* (what we do), missional *character* (how we do it), and missional *motivation* (why we do what we do). These four phrases best describe the purpose for which they have entered into a deliberate "process of change and transformation."

Looking back over the last five years (yes, the IMPACT congregations entered into this process only five years before our visit), one can see that their prayer, study, and intensive conversation and learning have led most of all to these results: (1) a clearer picture of the difficulty with which traditional establishment churches along the Atlantic seaboard make the change toward a community with a missional vocation, (2) a grasp of the issues that must be addressed to achieve faithful change, and (3) the renewal of focus on God's vision for the world and for the church instead of their own survival. These results have been born out of hard work and in turn bear the fruit of hope for the future! Perhaps the vocation of these churches, then — at least for now — is "discerning God's call."

Opportune Moments — The "*When* Are We?" Question

Hendrik Kraemer, a missionary leader of the middle of the twentieth century, once said, "Strictly speaking, one ought to say that the church is always in a state of crisis and that its greatest shortcoming is that it is only occasionally aware of it."[6] The Chinese character for *crisis,* we are told, is a combination of the characters for "danger" and "opportunity." Each moment presents the church with both, and that means always having to decide. What do we do now? What new opportunity and danger is facing us? What does faithfulness require in this time and place?

In a sense, what has already been said underscores the importance of time. The local particularities of a neighborhood, a city, a region, or a town are the fruit of their histories. They are what they are today, and that is different from what they were yesterday or what they will be tomorrow. To discern vocation in terms of place is also to discern it in terms of time.

But something else is important to notice in the churches we visited. That is the way in which there have been particular moments in their stories when the discernment happened. Sometimes those were sharply defined, decisive moments. Other times, it was more like the daily showers of a rainy season than a thunderstorm. Sometimes it caught their attention like a bolt of lightning. Other times it slipped in on them like the dawn of a new day or showed up more in the fading shadows of dusk — but was decisive, nonetheless.

Catalytic Moment

The arrival of the young priest, Father Bryan Karvelis, came at a time when the German-rooted life of Transfiguration Parish was at a low ebb and a

---

6. Hendrik Kraemer, *The Christian Message in a Non-Christian World* (London: Edinburgh House, 1947 [c. 1938]), p. 24.

fundamental re-rooting of congregational life had to take place. It was a moment when the situation demanded what a young, risk-taking priest brought by way of new vision. This was a critical moment for establishing the spirituality of Charles de Foucauld and the experiments in the forms of parish life that followed. A new direction commenced.

Not unlike that were the circumstances of Rockridge United Methodist Church in Oakland in 1988. The congregation was nearing the brink of death. Pastor David McKeithen was appointed to attempt to "revitalize" the church. Soon a team of six additional leaders came together who shared a vision. Influenced by Church of the Savior in Washington, DC, InterVarsity Christian Fellowship (a university ministry), and memories of the importance of Wesley's class meeting structure for discipleship accountability, a new direction was forged. It was a catalytic moment.

Rockridge sees its vocation in a way that is unique among the churches we visited. Its intent is to be a community of Mission Covenant Groups, and each of those groups is expected to discern its God-given vocation. Therefore, local responsibility is multiple, and the church's "turf" is a patchwork of places and social contexts where the groups live in missional covenant. But each part of the mosaic is vivid and strong because it is rooted so deeply in the commitments and bonds of a small, intentional group of disciples.

Each Mission Covenant Group at Rockridge devotes itself primarily to its respective neighborhood or social niche, and therefore each group has its own charism, its own organizing principle. One seeks to meet educational needs in the community through such means as an in-service workshop for teachers in the local school. Another is an artistic group that uses its talents in proclamation through "outdoor art," making an effort to draw disparate elements of the surrounding community together and get them talking to one another. Another group is working with people in the technology industry, and offers classes for people in the area who need to learn how to use computers. One Rockridge group builds homes for the poor in connection with Habitat for Humanity. A group made up of people from several different Mission Covenant Groups engaged in an experiment in communal housing. They purchased a plot of land and hired an architect to design such a place, incorporating separate apartments with shared community space that includes a kitchen and dining facility.

In the end, it is the overall vocation — and charism — of Rockridge to live "intently" with one another in missional accountability. And that bold experiment, which has not been without its difficulties, came about at a critical moment when it was possible to start down a new path.

Smoldering Vision

But a catalytic moment with the potential to focus a church's missional vocation is only one of the ways vocation becomes clear to a church. For other
churches we visited, discerning vocation emerged more out of instincts
that had been simmering for a long time. Somewhere beneath the surface,
at times showing up above the surface, certain perspectives and practices
seemed to smolder, waiting for the time when they would be fanned into
flame by something new in the situation or someone new in the mix. A
recognition of the church's calling comes to clarity as the church makes
the "obvious decision of the moment." Holy Ghost Church illustrates this
pattern: the mantra "love everybody," a prophetic utterance by a Nigerian
archbishop to "go to your Jerusalem," a search for an available facility in the
city and not out in the megachurch-supporting suburbs, a vision to "relo-
cate" into a community of need — a cluster of decisions, each leading to the
next. In the end, clarity about its calling.

The move to establish Eastbrook Church as a church in and for the
city of Milwaukee came from the instincts of a number of people. The story
you get about that depends on who you ask. Some will tell you they and
others at Elmbrook Church had the idea first and began meeting in their
homes within the city in anticipation of becoming a church there. They
talked with Elmbrook folks about allowing Marc Erickson, an MD and by
that time a key teacher in the Elmbrook Church, to come be their pastor-
preacher. If you ask Marc, it had come to be a vision of his to start a church
in the city, and that led to the initiative. If you ask others, they might tell
you that the Elmbrook pastor, Stuart Brisco, had the vision and approached
Marc to encourage him to start a city church. But no matter. The diversity of
stories tells us that there was general ferment in the direction of founding a
church with the vocation to *be* in the city. It coalesced into what Eastbrook
Church has come to be today.

As we have observed, Eastbrook's vocation is framed in terms of the
"city." In one sense, that is an intentionally broad sense of the locale of its
responsibility in mission. In its earlier years, it used worship and ministry
facilities that were located near the University of Wisconsin (Milwaukee)
campus. That particular neighborhood lent some of the character of what
it meant to be a church for the city, but the church's view was always larger
than a neighborhood. Its relationships and practices said it saw its vocation
larger than that, but never apart from it, either. This is illustrated by what
happened in the course of the church's move to new facilities in the late

1990s. After it outgrew the capacities of the prior facilities, a search was on for a new place. It was assumed this must be found within the city. One site was found, but in the end negotiations failed to establish proper zoning, so a further search was made. Finally, the church came to purchase the campus of a Roman Catholic parish that had merged with another. While this was now in a new section of the city, the city focus continued. But the city focus meant that whatever immediate neighborhood surrounded their facility was an important place to which they had a calling as well. One of the early initiatives among the people of the neighborhood was a weekday youth program. One couple, who were among some of the earliest members of Eastbrook, began to establish relationships with teenagers met through the new program and then with their families. Quickly they discerned how awkward it was for them to move along the streets and among the families of the neighborhood as people who lived some distance away. They noticed a duplex for sale and decided to buy it as "investment" property (double meanings are welcomed!). That gave them a reason to be there, and made them stakeholders in the welfare of the neighborhood. The tangible rootedness of their action is what makes commitment to "the city" more than a vague generality!

The missional vocation of the West Yellowstone Presbyterian Church sort of grew on them. There was no earthshaking moment of decision or revelation. It grew out of a long history. The church had come to play a certain role for the permanent-resident town and for the tourist-season resort. It had members and officers from among both groups of residents, and that kept focus on being faithful in both directions. It was during the time before the present co-pastors arrived that this sense of mission seemed to crystallize. During the period of pastoral search, it was in their prayers that the leaders were led toward this vision of being a town-tourist church. Something was dawning on them about how God had shaped them and where that was leading.

Conscious Reflection

For other churches, missional vocation grows out of a conscious process of reflection together about God's calling. It may be stimulated by changing circumstances surrounding the church, or a sense of aimlessness within, or nagging tugs from biblical images that haunt the church with another picture of the way things ought to be.

For the IMPACT churches, it was a sense of the growing distance between their character as churches and the nature of the world around them. That led them to band together in a new way as churches living out of a common heritage and facing a common situation. They committed themselves to a collective process seeking discernment. Together they have grappled with their Reformed heritage to know themselves better. They have studied their context to get to know the kinds of people who live in it and the fundamental assumptions people in their region live by. They have explored biblical themes that call into question assumptions and practices of the past and call into being new ones. By partnering together to read the context, identify the shaping factors of the heritage, and explore new moves to make, the pastors and key leaders of the churches are framing a new question for all in the congregations to learn to engage.

For the Spring Garden Church of Willowdale, in Toronto, the key word may well be "attentiveness." Spring Garden has for many years met and worshiped in a facility tucked into a residential neighborhood of Willowdale. Their building is only a few blocks from the business district and civic center of North York, an aggressive urban development on the north side of Toronto that is now incorporated into an expanded Metro Toronto. The neighborhood of the facility and adjoining neighborhoods have experienced further change by the onset of the phenomenon of the so-called monster homes, which are large extended-family dwellings displacing the smaller bungalow homes of the area.

What has been striking about Spring Garden is how they have given increasing attention to these things. John McLaverty, after eighteen years as their pastor, did extensive research into the social history by which the modern "edge city" of North York had come to be a new kind of urban space. Ethnographic interviews put him and the church in touch with Asian populations now finding their home in the area. As he learned, so did the other staff and officers of the church. This contextual "reality therapy" was matched with theological exploration into the nature and witness of the church. They joined the ferment around the notion of "missional church," which led them to see themselves in new ways. Ultimately, this meant forging a fresh notion guiding the roles of staff ("mission team") and of the pastor ("mission team leader"). It meant a congregation-wide reflection of the missional nature of the church. It meant developing a clearer idea of the church's mission ("Christ in the City"). Attentiveness to organizational styles and assumptions inherited by virtue of its being a Canadian Baptist church led to fresh patterns for encouraging the missional initiatives of all the members by setting a tone of freedom and spontaneity. Paths of conscious reflection on missional character have led to a predisposition to be responsive to concerns across the city in Christ's name and in Christ's way. They have become a people able to respond nimbly and quickly to each moment's opportunity.

In Bellevue, an affluent city just east of Seattle, First Presbyterian Church has enjoyed a long history as a metropolitan area church. Like many other large, West Coast, evangelical Presbyterian churches, it has the heritage of being a church with deep roots in biblical study and knowledge, commitment to personal evangelism, and involvement in the support of global mission efforts. Its style of worship is pastorally warm with a moderately classical style of hymnody and choral expression. When members are asked what drew them to this church, over and over again the response is "the pastor" (Dick Leon) and his thoughtful and personal preaching.

Like many churches of its style and size and age, Bellevue First faces the pressure to be a "full-service church" with well-run programs to serve the interests and needs of all potential attenders and members, of all ages and backgrounds. A large and efficient staff attests to the church's commitment to respond to that. But it is evident that in the midst of that there are rumblings about the shape and direction of this 2,500-member church, motivated by questions about its proper sense of vocation. The pastor in his preaching has worked to cultivate a "missional church" perspective for the church, and he has led the elders into intentional theological reflection on that theme and others crucial to their leadership. Program staff indicate a hunger for personal relationships among the people of the church beyond their program management assignments. Work is being done to establish small groups throughout the congregation as a fabric for cultivating community and discipleship. Extensive work is being done to train the 120 deacons for their important ministries of helps. The Alpha Course is being introduced as a way that hospitality-based evangelism can be done in the congregation. A high school completion program for dropouts from the school system is hosted in the church's facility. Full-orbed training for cross-cultural ministry is provided for members who are the congregation's agents in sister-church relationships and short-term mission ventures in specific parts of the world where continuing connections are being nurtured. In all of it, the discernment and engagement is done in the midst of the tension between a provider-of-goods-and-services orientation and the church's formation as a missional community with a clear sense of vocation.

Dialogue with Tradition — The "*Who* Are We?" Question

The churches we visited are rooted in different ecclesial traditions: United Methodist, Roman Catholic, Evangelical, Baptist, Presbyterian, Pentecostal, Mennonite, and Reformed. Those differences show up. They would be recognizable to anyone knowledgeable about the traditions in which they have been formed. But that is not the whole story. For each of them, discerning their missional vocation has inevitably meant having a fresh conversation with their tradition. They have had to ask questions about what in their tradition will nourish their missional vocation and what will hinder it. They have probed their traditions to discover untapped resources. They have drawn on their tradition, recovered it, and enhanced it. And they have also differentiated themselves from it at fundamental points, critiquing it and changing it. Vocational discernment has made it clearer to them that they have a tradition and that it is important to their missional identity today. And it has made it clearer to them that their missional engagement today tests and refines and reforms that tradition as new potentials in it are discovered.

The Boulder Mennonite Church in Colorado was especially challenged by the prospect of living its tradition in a seemingly inhospitable place. The church has found Boulder to be a very secular and very wealthy place. The New Age spiritualities popular there are not Mennonite spiritualities! A community formed around a Mennonite ethic of simplicity can be something of an oddity when it is plopped down in one of the ten wealthiest counties in the USA.

The challenge for the Boulder Church was to embody their inherited values within the social context in such a way that they would be made present and accessible to others. They would have to be the kind of community that sustained each other in lifestyle choices. They would have to work out a way not to be separatist in character, an affliction that sometimes affects communities with strong countercultural convictions. They would have to be more than a community that by virtue of its tradition *stood* for peace, and be a community that *enacted and contributed* peace. That was the challenge that would lead them to weave a tight connection between a theology of reconciliation and the practice of it. So, among other things, they initiated and pioneered the Victim-Offender Reconciliation Program (VORP).

The Mennonite tradition is strong, even for those who did not grow up in it and only encountered it once they came into this congregation. But its tangible styles have had to be formed in the crucible of God's calling and their social context. Some of that happens in their small groups. Each one discerns for itself its missional focus, and while there is some ambiguity about how all the groups' efforts are connected, several things seem to stand out. The concern for reconciliation and peacemaking is a major strand in it all. Also, the dedication to "meeting human needs" is prominent. And for a number of the groups, there is special concern for what goes on on "the hill."

"The hill" is a part of the city near the university that is the site of notable social protest and conflict. On hearing about the "rainbow kids" living on the streets on the hill and the pressures from store owners and others to have them removed, one of the small groups decided to make burritos to take to the kids. They got in the habit of it and continued for three months until finally the kids were run off. On another occasion there were mounting tensions between rioting students and police on the hill, and four or five members decided to go to the hill. There they walked cautiously but decidedly among the police and the students, offering themselves as a "third presence" in the interest of peace. These are examples of ways the church has learned to deal with their peace legacy as a mandate, as their vocation.

The small mission-oriented groups of the Boulder Church are similar to those of the Rockridge Church in Oakland. But in the case of Rockridge, the precedent for that is John Wesley's "class meeting," with its system of "class leaders." The retrieval of the accountability and focused discipleship of the class meeting structure is a conscious part of Rockridge's conversation with its heritage, a heritage buried deep in Methodism but in many respects lost to contemporary practice. But with some others within the United Methodist Church, Rockridge is intent on recovering from that lost tradition. Another recent tradition, the innovative form of community in the Church of the Savior in Washington, DC, is part of the mix as tradition sharpens tradition.

This dialogue with tradition(s) has not been painless, of course. The commitment of the leadership to focus the church around Mission Covenant Groups has not met with universal approval in the church. The difficulty of winding up with two tiers of membership — the group-participating members and the worship-attending members — has yet to be resolved in practice. But even the difficulty constitutes a dialogue with numerous renewal traditions in the history of the Christian church that have come up against similar problems.

As it is a Roman Catholic parish, certain features of organization and liturgical practice at Transfiguration are fixed. The parish does not have, nor would it want to have, the measure of local choice that even congregations within mainline Protestant denominations have, let alone the local autonomy of churches in a Baptist polity or independent churches. And yet, within the tradition there are traditions that provide possibilities for innovative approaches to community, leadership, and liturgy. Particularly, the spirituality of Charles de Foucauld and the patterns of the Base Ecclesial Communities of Latin America are overlays on the fixed structures that have become an inherent part of the missional fabric of the congregation.

The effort at Transfiguration has been to generate a kind of discipleship that combines aspects of the traditional Catholic parish with what it means to be an intentional community. This touches the organizational structure of the parish. The focus on intentional community has been most apparent in the work to sustain the strong network of fraternities — small Christian communities within the parish that meet in homes throughout the area. The responsibles who lead them, by their weekly meditation, worship, discernment, and planning together on Saturday mornings, have become the center of decision making for the parish. The responsibles have come to function as the parish council.

The celebration of the mass contains a homily that has been influenced by the ways the fraternities engaged the same lectionary texts during the preceding week. It is the intention of Father Bryan to use the mass to relate Christ to the contemporary situation of the congregation. He sees it as a liturgical framework for contextual communication, so liturgy is adapted to the lives of the people. The sanctuary itself reflects the core commitments. The chancel has been stripped of the ornate, and in its place are bare symbols appropriate to the spirituality the community is called to follow: to be present with Christ in the Eucharist, and present with the poorest of the poor.

An interesting mixture of traditions converges in what Holy Ghost Church is today. A visit to their annual Founders Day celebration helps to sort out the various strands. Worship pastor Val McCune is the team historian, and she provides a historical map, with pictures and notations to highlight the people who embodied the various traditions from which they have grown. This includes leaders in the Missionary Baptist and National Baptist traditions who first formed the church in the 1940s and led it through its early years. It includes early founding leaders of what came to be called Pentecostalism, a stream that has come into the life of Holy Ghost in recent decades (marked by the addition of "Full Gospel" to the church's name). It includes American and African leaders in the International Communion of Charismatic Churches with which the church is associated. Even beyond what makes it onto the formal map, the church's character is shaped by traditions such as the ministry approach of John Perkins and the Voice of Calvary and the liturgical renewal influences of Robert Webber.

Along with the shaping influence of all these traditions comes a necessary dialogue at critical points. In particular, the church sees itself at odds with choices made by many companions within African-American Pentecostal and Baptist circles who have seemed to exchange the message of deliverance and holiness for one of health and wealth. The connection with Nigeria places the church in relationship with churches like the one there that recently opened a 50,000-seat sanctuary and had 40,000 in worship on the first Sunday! The natural instinct toward self-questioning (Why isn't this happening here?) and self-doubt (Why isn't God blessing us that way?) sets afoot another kind of dialogue. It forces the church to know its own environment better and to see the difference between the cultures of America and Nigeria at the present moment. It brings to sharper relief the differences in spiritual hunger, fundamental worldview, and religious moods. The post-Christian character of American sensibilities and the religious consumerism of an individualistic society become new factors that confirm the church's commitment to refuse to pitch the church to what would draw the crowds in today's Detroit.

The city location and focus of Eastbrook's life has meant it has become different from its parent Elmbrook Church. But the difference is not total. The theological heritage and evangelical cast of the church's life and style have roots there that remain evident. Identifying the threads of traditions held and valued within the congregation is evident at two special points. Along the way, Pastor Marc Erickson has prepared extensive notes on theological themes important to the leadership of the church, showing their continuities with a full range of ecclesial traditions, including not only evangelical and Protestant but Roman Catholic and Eastern Orthodox traditions. He attempts to show the whole family tree and the church's relation to it. The effort is certainly part of the church's impulse to value and be in partnership with churches of all sorts in the city and not to conceive of itself as an isolated, self-sufficient church. Also, the worship leadership, during the early years of the church, gave serious attention to the development of a theology of worship. The fruit of that work still remains the touchstone, and the theology that orients worship shows the marks of dialogue with a number of traditions, many of which have come into this "independent, community church" in the memories and practices of members whose prior church experience was in congregations of other denominations, including mainline Protestant churches and the Roman Catholic Church.

For some of the churches we visited, the dialogue with tradition is not so much with what we would normally understand to be the distinctiveness of their particular denominational traditions, theological or liturgical. Rather, it is with the accumulated patterns of "being an organization" that have shaped the way things are done in North American churches in general. This seems to be the case with Spring Garden, where there is a certain caution about or distance from the accepted ways of operating assumed within the Canadian Baptist system of which it is a part. The issue is, "How are we supposed to be the church?" and the established answers to that question are challenged by Spring Garden's pursuit of a lifestyle that plays out a missional understanding of the church and the present context in which the church lives.

In similar fashion, the Reformed churches of the IMPACT group and the Presbyterian churches in West Yellowstone and Bellevue dialogue not only with their Reformed heritage but with the more recent experience of Reformed and other mainline denominations that has to do with organizational form. Many scholars have demonstrated that fundamental operating assumptions of the twentieth-century church — denominationally and congregationally — have formed under the shaping influence of American corporate styles.[7] These churches wrestle, sometimes more consciously and sometimes less, with the way values such as economy of scale, efficiency, rational order and control, division of labor, and specialization have left us with a kind of church that is more like a "vendor of religious services and goods" than a "body of people sent on a mission."[8] The dialogue is at points more emphatically an engagement with American pragmatic traditions than it is with a particular ecclesial and theological tradition.

Continuous Cultivation — The "*Why* Are We?" Question

A congregation's sense that it has a missional vocation, and its idea of what that vocation is, come about out of the crucible of struggle. The circum-

7. See for example Milton J Coalter, John M. Mulder, and Louis B. Weeks, eds., *The Organizational Revolution*, The Presbyterian Presence, vol. 6 (Louisville: Westminster/John Knox, 1991).

8. See Guder, *Missional Church*, pp. 33-37, 49-51, and 76-77.

stances of the church's context, the resources (and liabilities) of the church's tradition, and the voice of God in the biblical word are all part of the mix. Discernment emerges in multiple ways, but always these are the crucial factors.

But discernment and vocation are not one-time matters. Discerning is a constant challenge, as is following. Yesterday's discernments are met by today's new questions and visions. So it is important to notice in the churches we visited how they cultivate and nourish their sense of missional vocation in continuing ways.

When a church like Holy Ghost takes up residence in a neighborhood — their personal residence as well as the place where their gatherings reside — the continuous cultivation comes pretty naturally. Their vocation is the neighborhood, and they're always there! They're on the streets, in the homes, and along the alleyways. They are *present* to the neighborhood, and they're a part of the neighborhood. So the vocation stays vivid.

In addition, the strong bonds among the group of pastors and elders and the synergy of their various ministries continue to nurture vision at the center. If an aspect of that fades, once noticed it is quickly rebuilt, because core leadership people are around. Their lives intertwine. Newer leadership is consciously drawn into the central dynamic that sets the tone for the whole.

Spring Garden has the habit of praying, and on periodic occasions they do that together on a Saturday morning "prayer walk." Sometimes as many as one hundred of them will gather, and in smaller clusters walk the streets of the urban strip a few blocks away, or the neighborhood bungalows, or the newer monster homes, praying as they go. They pray for shopkeepers, for civic officials, for corporations, for older residents on fixed income, for young families starting out, for wealthy new Asian immigrants, for whoever comes to their attention as they walk and watch and listen. This habit keeps them in touch with what their study has identified. But it keeps it personal. It keeps it up to date. It keeps it vivid, fixing the direction of their vocation.

In Spring Garden, missional team leader John McLaverty plays the important role of continuing to focus the energy of the congregation. But he doesn't do that by setting the agenda for them. He creates a climate where that can happen. He practices at the center the value placed on the readiness to respond with spontaneity and grace.

Eastbrook Church had from the beginning a clear direction. They were to be a church of, and in, and for the city. Particular expressions of that have always had to be worked out. But clarity about what guides the choices has been maintained. To the present time, the "city-ness" of their vocation is a topic that calls forth the conversation about what God wants them to do.

The vision is maintained because the central values it entails are over and over again articulated and demonstrated and rehearsed. The community practices what it means to be a church for the city. They perform that central conviction at every opportunity.

As might be expected, Pastor Marc plays a large role in keeping the core story alive and tangible. For example, the unity with other churches which is so large a part of how Eastbrook sees itself as a church for the city is expressed in numerous ways in Marc's comments, illustrations, communications, attitudes and actions. There is no mistaking how much of a core value this is for him as well as the church. But Marc is not alone. Worship leadership, for example, sets the tone from the very beginning in the worship gatherings. They serve notice: "We are in partnership with Christ's other churches in the city and we do not seek or encourage people to leave those churches to join us here."

In a more direct and deliberate way, the Rockridge Church and the Boulder Church maintain continuous attention on the matter of discerning missional vocation by expecting that in each of the small groups. That of course requires nurturing and accountability, but their groups function at high levels in the practice of discernment.

The Boulder Church takes that one step farther. In addition to what the groups do regarding their own particular mission focus, the whole congregation is gathered in retreat once a year for what is called "mapmaking," an exercise of ministry discernment. They ask, "What is our ministry? Who are we? What are we about?" The purpose is to keep the central mission vision of the congregation lively and refreshed, and to ensure that the vision is pressed into the fabric of all the activities of the church.

In a similar fashion, Transfiguration has built into its rhythm of life occasions for continuing to ask the discernment questions. In one way, this is a weekly routine. The fraternities read the lectionary texts and ask how this informs their vocation and shapes them for it. The responsibles meet weekly with each other and Father Bryan, and together they seek to discern the voice of the Spirit through the Scriptures and through their contemplation of Christ in the Eucharist. But then, every six months the responsibles go on retreat together for an extended time. Their primary purpose is to discern what the congregation needs to hear during the next half year. It is an exercise in anticipating what God wants to say to them next and how that will lead them in their vocation. Out of this discernment, the agenda for the small fraternities is set.

Vocation and Charism

The term *charism* is an English rendering of the New Testament Greek word for "gift," and it has to do with the gifts the Holy Spirit gives to Christian believers. The "gifts" are practices and abilities specially given to each to be used for the common good of the Christian community, and they are the means for ministering the grace of Christ to one another. And at least once in the New Testament, the word *gifts* is used in reference to those special persons given to the community for equipping all for the work of ministry (Eph. 4:10-11). Roman Catholics use the term *charism* to speak about these gifts. Protestants tend to use the language of "spiritual gifts."

Here we are daring to suggest that just as the term *vocation* can be used of congregations, so can *charism*. There is precedent for this in Roman Catholic usage, as when a religious order or community is said to have a particular charism, that is, a special gift which they offer to the whole Christian community. It is tied closely to the vocation of such a community, something they have especially been called to do on behalf of the whole church. It is in that sense that we have used the word *charism* in reference to the churches we have visited. Their charism is that unique trait, that particular feature of the congregation's life and contribution that comes from the exercise of the vocation they have discerned to be theirs.

To illustrate: For half a dozen years in the 1970s, I was pastor of the Covenant Presbyterian Church of Biloxi, Mississippi. That fairly new and small congregation found itself, little by little, ministering in a range of ways among children and teenagers. That was not only because of the high proportion of teenagers in the families of the church. There were other factors. For one thing, the teenagers of the church's families brought in many of their peers, and that swelled the youth group. But also, a number of families in the church, somewhat independently of each other at first, began to volunteer at the local youth court. That involved things like extended care for infants awaiting the outcome of custody matters, weekend care for delinquent teenagers awaiting the adjudication of their cases, or big brother / big sister relationships with troubled kids. At points it involved formal adoption into one of the families of the church. It also involved points of advocacy for children within the community. But there had never been a formal decision that children and youth were the church's missional calling, or that the church thought it had that spiritual gift. It simply emerged as a characteristic response of the church to what seemed to be important to God. What emerged was something like the charism of that church.

What we have identified as the charism of each of these churches we visited is intimately linked to the vocation they have discerned and followed. As is the case with an individual's spiritual gifts, or charisms, a congregation's recognition of its charism derives from the faithful fulfillment of its vocation. To be called to a particular vocation does not necessarily mean that God sends us to do what we feel we are good at, what we are gifted for, or what we would enjoy doing. Biblical accounts of callings illustrate that the more normal pattern is that callings tend to involve the same forms of suffering and sacrifice that Jesus' calling did. The gift of the Spirit to fulfill the calling comes in the course of the faithful response. It becomes evident only over time what that gift, that charism, has been. Once evident, its presence in the pulse of a congregation's life is a gift to the whole church toward the fulfillment of its missional nature. And, in fact, it is a gift from God to the world that is coming to know Christ because this charism has come to expression in this congregation that takes its vocation seriously.

> The calling of the church to be missional — to be a sent community — leads the church to step beyond the given cultural forms that carry dubious assumptions about what the church is, what its public role should be, and what its voice should sound like. Testing and revising our assumptions and practices against a vision of the reign of God promises the deep renewal of the missional soul of the church that we need. By daily receiving and entering the reign of God, through corporate praying for its coming and longing for its appearance, and in public living under its mantle, this missional character of the church will be nourished and revived.[9]

9. See Guder, *Missional Church*, p. 109.

Renewing a Public Voice

2006

I am fairly certain that, in the way it has come to be understood since Martin Marty coined the term in reference to Reinhold Niebuhr,[1] I would not be mistaken for a "public theologian." I am a mission theologian. And I am an ecclesiologist — a theologian of the church. But I know that pursuing a healthy missiology and ecclesiology means that I am engaged in "public theologizing." The mission requires it. The church's sense of its identity and calling requires it. The God who birthed the church and its mission intends it.

The particular avenues along which my work as missiologist and ecclesiologist has traveled most are those precipitated by Lesslie Newbigin's now-familiar challenge from the 1980s onward, that there needs to be "a missionary encounter of the gospel with our Western culture." The North American Gospel and Our Culture Network (GOCN), whose work I have been privileged to coordinate,[2] exists as a movement in which thousands of people seek collaborative ways of responding to that challenge. The image of "gospel and culture encounter" has shared space in that movement with the image of the "missional church," a church implicated in the gospel-and-culture encounter and sent in the midst of the world on those terms.

The public theologizing made necessary by the GOCN agenda is underscored by the network's discoveries as it has attended to the historically shifting social location of the church and the impact that has on the church's

---

1. See Martin E. Marty, "Reinhold Niebuhr: Public Theology and the American Experience," *Journal of Religion* 54, no. 4 (October 1974): 332-59.

2. [Ed. note: The author coordinated the GOCN from its 1987 beginnings through 2010.]

character and witness. To reiterate what has become a familiar litany, we have noted the following:

1. The relegation of religious faith — which in the case of the USA meant Protestant Christian faith, mainly — to the private realm of permitted options, assigned to the private, family, and leisure areas of life and set outside the public ranges of life as having no direct bearing. This has been chronicled by Martin Marty, Alasdair MacIntyre, Lesslie Newbigin, and many others.
2. The shift in recent decades from what remained of the church's privileged chaplaincy role in the social and public space. The society's former eagerness to receive the moral fruit of the church's influence on private life, forming character and values for those who would take up roles in public office or commercial enterprise, has waned and pretty much vanished. In Vigen Guroian's words, "we are witnessing the end of the symbiotic relationship of biblical faith and society. . . . The day of American Christendom is over."[3]
3. The failing confidence in modernity's reliance on autonomous reason, its epistemological certainty, its privileging of individual choice and self-interest, and its faith in progress — technological and social. In modernity's place, yet in mixed and ambiguous form, there have arisen postmodern sensibilities corresponding to what has come to be called the "postmodern condition."

Within my own work, and perhaps in the GOCN movement's emphasis more broadly, I fear that the public dimensions of the agenda have been too little attended to. It may justifiably be said that the movement has tended to be more quietistic, or perhaps simply institution-bound (working within the churches as currently configured to be local organizations and/or corporate denominations). There are notable exceptions, colleagues within the network who have worked deliberately on the public dimensions of the agenda, including Charles West, Barry Harvey, Gary Simpson, and Bill Wylie-Kellermann, to name just a few. Within the range of the network's reflections, however, it is important to note some very significant trajectories among the accents and visions of the movement that open up potentially fruitful conversation between missiology and the field of inquiry

---

3. Vigen Guroian, *Ethics after Christendom: Toward an Ecclesial Christian Ethic* (Grand Rapids: Eerdmans, 1994), pp. 95, 12.

that has been dubbed "public theology." Neither of these fields has tended to see itself implicated in the concerns of the other, and each is impoverished by its distance from the other. By seizing and expanding upon some of the accents in the "gospel and our culture" conversation, we may be able to open up new ground for exploring cross-discipline possibilities.

One of the most important themes in the GOCN movement is the recovery of the central place of the reign of God in the message of Jesus — i.e., his gospel. "Turn around and believe this good news," he said, "the reign of God is at hand!" The identity of his followers, the rationale for being church, the spilling out of this news report everywhere, were all bound up in this fundamentally new moment, one that provided the clue to the meaning of history and a vision of the world's true destiny. News such as this was by its nature public. It is, as Lesslie Newbigin put it, "public truth."[4] It belongs to the whole world, then and now. This announcement of the reign of God, and the reality of its presence in Jesus Christ, capture us with a sense of what the public good is and can be, and makes witnesses out of us. We have tasted what God intends the world to be like in the end, and that opens a new way of being with everyone in that world. This is not a private, inner, personal faith, but a shaping story that implicates us into God's mission. Touched by the recovery of the theme, many are recognizing the major shift it brings about for contemporary, self-interest-oriented, consuming Americans. We dare not any longer view salvation in terms of what we acquire in the transaction, but rather hear Jesus' call to mean participation — we have been laid hold of for the larger purposes of God, and those purposes touch the whole range of issues that have to do with public life.[5]

"Public" is a word that lurks at every turn in our emerging missional ecclesiology. The word *ekklesia* itself is drawn not from first-century Greek terminology for the variety of acceptable salvation cults, but from the idea of a civic meeting. Like its Hebrew counterpart *(qahal)* it "refers originally to a deliberative assembly of the body politic."[6] *Ekklesia* means "called into public assembly," a town meeting, the gathered public. "As God calls the whole world to its proper worship in public assembly, we can think of the church as the community that has thus far assembled. It lives its life, there-

4. See especially Lesslie Newbigin, *Truth to Tell: The Gospel as Public Truth* (Grand Rapids: Eerdmans, 1991).

5. Cf. James V. Brownson, Inagrace T. Dietterich, Barry A. Harvey, and Charles C. West, *StormFront: The Good News of God* (Grand Rapids: Eerdmans, 2003).

6. John Howard Yoder, *The Christian Witness to the State* (Eugene, OR: Wipf and Stock, 1998 [c. 1964]), p. 18.

fore, in public and for the public."[7] "Public" is associated with the New Testament word *kerygma* and its verbal counterparts. Usually translated "preaching," it has nothing to do with what we now call preaching — a homily or exposition or sermon given in the context of (usually) Sunday worship. Its meaning field has to do with the function of the "herald," the news announcement by the official spokesvoice of one in power or authority. The public broadcast of the news, the "*public* action" of it, is the form of witness the New Testament describes.

Worship, too, is public. It is not public merely in the sense that the doors are open to the public and all are welcome to enter and join in. As Vigen Guroian notes, following Parker Palmer, this is very little "public" when the openness to the public is to join a very private-oriented faith in a private-faith-oriented community's gathered worship.[8] Even that may be too generous because what happens most is a worship setting orchestrated to allow persons entering the space and ambiance and ingredients to be able to worship. That's a far cry from "gathered worship." Even to use such a phrase as "gathered worship" says more! It says worship is generated out of all the experience of God in the public ranges of life that motivate and shape the worship a community brings with it into a common gathering.

The Greek word from which we derive our word "liturgy" has public, missional significance at its root. *Leitourgia* had to do with public service, usually rendered at one's own expense. It was not about "the work of the people" as we have tended to take it. It was about a "work for the people" — for the broader range of people who are the objects of God's love and dreams, the whole public! In its liturgy, the church is a community for the whole.[9]

The public nature of the church's identity, its message, and its vocation of worship and witness, places the people of God squarely in the public life of the world. While the ethos of many (most?) congregations in our part of the world fails to reflect that, simple observation confirms it. Once we are clear that "church" is not an organization to which one belongs but a body of people sent, once we are clear on who we are, then where we are is not the facility on the corner but people pressed into the fabric of life, living it in all the public dimensions shared by others. We are in the public every day. As

7. Linford L. Stutzman and George R. Hunsberger, "The Public Witness of Worship," in *Treasure in Clay Jars: Patterns in Missional Faithfulness*, Lois Y. Barrett et al., pp. 100-116 (Grand Rapids: Eerdmans, 2004), p. 105.

8. Guroian, *Ethics after Christendom*, p. 99.

9. Cf. Mark R. Francis, CSV, "Liturgy," in *Dictionary of Mission*, ed. Karl Müller, Theo Sundermeier, Stephen Bevans, and Richard Bliese (Maryknoll, NY: Orbis, 1999), pp. 284-85.

John Howard Yoder notes, we earn our living and raise our kids alongside of everyone else.[10]

This shapes three defining affirmations.

1. Public theologizing is missiological. That is to say that it is the church's missional calling that this be evident in its life. But it is also to say that public theologizing is not outside that calling as though another activity. All that is true of how mission must unfold touches and implicates public theologizing as well.

2. Public theologizing is the work of the whole people of God. It is not only the provenance of the professional theologian, nor the professional social ethicist or political theorist, nor the social or political activist. Nor is it assigned locally to the theologically trained clergy. All these, by their special ways of attending to public theology, give help to the people of God for this vocation. But the vocation remains theirs. This, in part, is why I have used the word "theologizing" instead of "theology." It is not a finished product, professional or otherwise, so much as an essential and ongoing practice of the missional church.

3. Public theologizing is done in a wide range of places. To talk about the public square begs for recognition that there are many publics and a variety of squares around which people work out matters of the common good. It includes what is normally in mind for most North Americans at the mention of the phrase: matters of governance, social policy, and politics. It includes other arenas as well:
   - economic interactions, exchanges, and transactions
   - workworld cultures and their particular orientations
   - media construals of reality, and the impact of their metanarratives and storylines
   - societal norms, bases for evaluating action, and preferences for behavior
   - ethnic communities, and their distinct nuances and patterns of relationship.

All these are arenas in which definitions of what it means to be human and to be a society are at stake. And these are where the Christian com-

10. Yoder, *Christian Witness.*

munity lives its daily presence, hence its habitual prayer for the nourishing bread of God's tomorrow to be ours to eat and share today.

Certainly, for the sake of encouraging this churchly practice, we need to bring to bear cultural and social analysis, ethics and particularly social ethics, concern for the daily occupation of all the people of God and its relation to their mission, and general concern for the church to find ways to move beyond the residual Constantinian scripts we carry in our collective memory, and the temptations that are so close at hand to hanker for a return of a privileged social status for our visions of the common good. What I propose to do here is a modest contribution in the midst of all of that. I wish to attend to the matter of the voice and posture in which Christians are present in and for public theologizing.

Experience in human relationships provides plenty of evidence that it isn't always *what* you say that is most important, but the *way* you say it. In fact, the way something is said itself tells the message. We who live on this side of Marshall McLuhan have heard this all before. "The medium is the message." (Or, if you prefer the book title, *The Medium Is the Massage.*[11])

I discovered this once while working in Luke's gospel. You have to feel it in the text of Luke 1 because printed words alone don't tell the whole story. The angel Gabriel comes first to Zachariah while he is performing his temple service. "Your wife Elizabeth will bear a son," he says. Zachariah asks, "How will I know that this is so? For I am an old man, and my wife is getting on in years." A few months later Gabriel visits Mary and tells her, "You will conceive in your womb and bear a son," to which she replies, "How can this be, since I am a virgin?" On the face of it, their responses to Gabriel were not that much different. Each voiced facts that made the announced birth counter-intuitive. The slight variance in their responses — "How will I know that this is so?" and "How can this be?" — doesn't prepare us for the sharp difference made in the assessment of what's taking place in their words. To Zachariah, Gabriel says, "Because you did not believe my words, you will become mute." To Mary, Elizabeth a little while later says, "Blessed is she who believed that there would be a fulfillment of what was spoken to her by the Lord" (Luke 1:45). Similar reactions, a world of difference in the matter of their belief. What made the difference? Was Gabriel hearing a different accent or tone of voice from each of them? Was there a different gesture or facial expression? Was there some attitude, more fundamental

11. Marshall McLuhan and Quentin Fiore, *The Medium Is the Massage: An Inventory of Effects* (New York: Bantam Books, Random House, 1967).

than the form of words, that was showing up in some subtle way? You had to be there, I expect.

Today, by the confluence of a radically changed social position and a long overdue recovery of missional identity as the people of God, we are faced with a similar kairos moment in the life and witness of the churches of the West in which our expressions (the ones in words) and our "expressions" (the ones in tones of voice and personal posture) will need to find a new inner resonance. Nowhere is our attentiveness to matters of voice and posture more necessary than in our public theologizing. By the character of our verbal and personal presence, by walking and standing and speaking in a new way, with new accents, we will make clear the way the reign of God in Jesus Christ presents itself to today's world.

I would like to position what I say about voice and posture against the backdrop of some lines of tension that may help to sharpen what it is we are searching for.

1. *The recovery of voice.* What kind of recovery we think we need depends on what we believe has been there before and what has somehow been lost. Several articulations offered in the early to mid-1990s illustrate the point. In 1995, Keith Clements published in the UK his book, *Learning to Speak.*[12] The idea of *learning* to speak is suggestive that a voice must be found. Ronald Thiemann suggests that more directly when he asks how we may "regain a public voice in our pluralistic culture." Something has been lost and is in need of recovery. In the end, Thiemann identifies the deeper issue by saying that this is a "search for an *authentic* public voice."[13]

At about the same time, comments by an American ethicist, Steve Hoogerwerf, carry a slightly different feel. Describing "virtues for Christian engagement in the public square," he includes these among them: "Moving from public proclamation as an imposition of values to public witness as a *bold* and *humble* invitation. Being *tolerant* because we're humble about our grasp of the gospel, not because we sacrifice our conviction about it being true. Being *hospitable* (welcoming strangers to be themselves) in the public square when we think we're right and they think we're wrong."[14] I value Hoogerwerf's thoughtful and sensitive contribution. But ten years later

12. Keith W. Clements, *Learning to Speak: The Church's Voice in Public Affairs* (Edinburgh: T&T Clark, 1995).

13. Ronald F. Thiemann, *Constructing a Public Theology* (Louisville, KY: Westminster/John Knox Press, 1991), pp. 19, 18 (emphasis mine).

14. Steve Hoogerwerf, printed notes accompanying a public lecture in 1994 given at Western Theological Seminary in Holland, Michigan.

there is something about it that feels anachronistic. Hoogerwerf works out of concern that the Christian public voice needs to get used to a new pluralist environment, to accommodate its voice and posture to that. It posits letting the "other" voices in, and even hosting the voice of the "other" in the public square. This presumes that Christians are those who up till now are in charge, and in new circumstances must now begin to make room. This feels very different from a quest to find our voice for entering the public space where the terms for engagement are already owned and shaped by other forces and voices.

So are we *modifying* our voice as we *give space* to others, or are we *seeking* a voice by which to *enter?* In every context, I suspect, there will be a unique mix.

2. *The recovery of the church's identity.* Here I have in mind representatives of another axis of tension we need to negotiate: Stanley Hauerwas and William Willimon on the one hand, and Lesslie Newbigin on the other. Their respective books published in the mid- to late 1980s, *Resident Aliens*[15] and *Foolishness to the Greeks,*[16] were seminal in the foundations of the GOCN movement in North America. The two visions share many things in common, particularly a concern for the churches to recover genuine and overt Christian character. In many respects, their ecclesiologies have convergence. If there is a difference — whether subtle or substantial — it grows from the soil of their different angles of concern about the present situation in which the churches of the West, and particularly North America, find themselves. They see different sides of the problem.

Hauerwas and Willimon see the problem as the over-accommodation of the churches, such that they have been little more than civic clubs (or country clubs), mildly religious at best, but embodying nothing distinctly different from the going visions and ideologies inherent in citizenship. So they call for the church to be again a distinctly and demonstrably Christian — and therefore cruciform — community. Newbigin, on the other hand, focuses on the cultural shifts by which the Christian faith has been relegated to the private realm in such a way that religious "belief" has come to be considered merely personal opinion with little or no relevance in public discourse. So his call for how the church can know, what the church must

15. Stanley Hauerwas and William H. Willimon, *Resident Aliens: Life in the Christian Colony* (Nashville: Abingdon Press, 1989).
16. Lesslie Newbigin, *Foolishness to the Greeks: The Gospel and Western Culture* (Grand Rapids: Eerdmans, 1986).

do, and who the church must be seeks the church's re-entry into its mission to be witnesses to the very public announcement of God's reign and Christ's lordship.

Which tug shall our voice and posture reflect? Are we shaped by the recovery of ecclesial practices by which we *are* a social ethic? Are we shaped by the recovery of missional practices by which we *testify* in action and word to the coming reign of God? I suggest that finding an authentic voice and posture lies somewhere within this tension and that our voice and posture are finally tested by both accents.

I propose, then, five features to orient our voice and posture in public theologizing.

A Spirit of Companionship

God so loved the world. As we walk among others in a pluralist social environment, what people will read very quickly is whether we stand aloof, or as one of them. Do we posture ourselves as over against them, or as a community that, while following a distinct vision, is nonetheless committed to the good of all? Has God fashioned us to oppose them, or to be on their side, even when we disagree? Do we carry ourselves as though we are somehow set outside their experience, as though we are the privileged few?

The line of difficulty involved in this comes from the fact that we do recognize that God has touched us to be the "aftertaste of God's loving triumph on the cross and foretaste of His ultimate loving triumph in His Kingdom."[17] Our posture reflects our fundamental ecclesiology: Are we a community of Christ for our own sakes? Or, with God for the sake of the world? If the latter, we owe companionship.

Previously, I have suggested that the church should see itself as sitting on both sides of the gospel-culture encounter (see above, pp. 101-8). We might be tempted to assume quickly that we are on the gospel side, but it is more crucial that we see ourselves first on the culture side in the encounter. The gospel meets our culture — the one we share with all others who are like us — within our own embodiment of it, in a continuing conversion like that about which Darrell Guder has so forcefully spoken.[18] The point

17. Yoder, *Christian Witness*, p. 10.
18. Darrell L. Guder, *The Continuing Conversion of the Church* (Grand Rapids: Eerdmans, 2000).

is that we are not removed from the simple reality that, as people who are part of a particular society, we share that society's cultural ways. When the gospel addresses our culture — whichever that is for each of us — it does so first by addressing us who inhabit that culture's worldview and ethos but have somewhere along the line said "yes" to Jesus' call to follow. It is only by virtue of that kind of continuing encounter that we are formed to be a people who inhabit the gospel's rendering of things. In that sense we sit on the gospel side, being for others in the society the 'hermeneutic' of the gospel by which they see it taking shape within their own culture.

The point of this is that for us to be the church does not disturb the fundamental companionship we have with others in our social environment. It remains that we are, like all others, the creations of God, made in God's likeness. *With* them we share common ways to see the world and interpret experiences in it and assign value and make judgments. *For* them, we have had all those things shaken and re-patterned by this news that the reign of God has come. But we are still one of them. Our voice should reflect that, and not carry the tone that presumes we are so other as to have nothing in common with them.

Raymond Fung makes this point with great force in his big little book *The Isaiah Vision.*[19] He offers a profoundly simple "ecumenical strategy for congregational evangelism" that has three movements. First, we work for those things identified in the Isaiah agenda as things God wants for this world. That agenda, drawn from Isaiah 65, simply envisions that God intends a world where infants do not die, old people have dignity, and working men and women enjoy the fruit of their labors. We work for that, and do so with anyone else who cares about the same things. And many people do! Next, we invite all who work alongside us, and all for whom we are working, to worship with us the God whose vision this is. Finally, we invite folks who have joined us into discipleship, to be followers of Jesus.

The core spirituality that Fung holds up in this model is one of partnership and solidarity. He invites us to be unafraid to work in companionship with any who will. "Comradeship" is a similar word whose root meaning may lend a helpful image. The word comes from the Middle French word *camarade* which refers to "a group that sleeps in the same room," referring often to soldiers quartered in a common barracks. As a globalizing world reminds us daily, we have the experience today of inhabiting "one

19. Raymond Fung, *The Isaiah Vision: An Ecumenical Strategy for Congregational Evangelism* (Geneva: WCC Publications, 1992).

room." That is true of our life with all others. That is true in particular ways of our life with all those with whom we share a common history and society and culture.

We dare not stand as though aloof. Charles West reminds us that "the powers are part of God's creation." We do not live over against them as the enemies of God's intent, but care for them as God does, even when, as is perennially the case, "the powers are not content to serve God." We, along with all others, are "caught up in this battle between God and the powers because we are the battleground."[20]

At many points in public discourse and action about the common good we will commend vision we believe to be God's. Many times there will be people who oppose that vision or have another vision to propose. In those encounters there remains a fundamental companionship at the heart of our relationship with others in the public square. The required posture is one that refuses to act or speak aloof from others who do not share the vision of our faith. Rather we walk with the grace of a comrade among those who sleep in the same barracks with us!

Humility in Truth-Telling

The gospel's truth is announced not so much in our personal evangelism's "tellings" of it as in our public theologizing expressions of its relevance to the public life of the world. It is just that kind of gospel! That requires humility and respectful styles of dialogue.

Lesslie Newbigin's articulation of what he called "proper confidence" has provided many people a way to restore confidence in their believing, even in public arenas that have their way of ruling out religious faith as so private as to be irrelevant to the public world of facts.[21] The form of knowledge in which we can have confidence, Newbigin says, is not the certainty sought in modernity. After all, knowing God is to know a person, and personal knowledge, as Newbigin learned long ago from Michael Polanyi, comes not by the exercise of a knower's autonomous rationality but by way of the self-disclosure of the one known. That, he says, is what we encounter

20. Brownson et al., *StormFront*, pp. 87, 89. Cf. Charles C. West, *Power, Truth, and Community in Modern Culture* (Harrisburg, PA: Trinity Press International, 1999).

21. Lesslie Newbigin, *Proper Confidence* (Grand Rapids: Eerdmans, 1995). Cf. Lesslie Newbigin, *The Gospel in a Pluralist Society* (Grand Rapids: Eerdmans, 1989), pp. 1-65.

in the Bible which he takes to be "that body of literature which — primarily but not only in narrative form — renders accessible to us the character and actions and purposes of God."[22]

But such a "proper confidence" as Newbigin describes must always have as its companion humility. We know in part, and all our knowing is qualified by the limitations of one vantage point and the distortions of human sin. We do not speak as though truth itself is what we utter. Rather, we recognize we are what I have elsewhere called a "community of the true" (see above, pp. 79-82). That is to say, we recognize Jesus to be the truth, and following him we are intent on being — in our forms of thinking and speaking and acting — *true* to that. That is, our ambition is to correspond to the truth. Our way of being that truth and our way of speaking that truth will be particular to who we are, what our cultural character is, and how we have thus far embodied that truth. Like every other Christian community in its own unique setting, we seek to be true to the One who *is* Truth.

This gives us the proper humility not to presume or propose more than that. In our various points of public engagement, our truth-telling is violated when in our voicing of what we know of the truth we convey that we so possess the truth that our expression of it is that very truth. Our accent and tone tell the truth better when they acknowledge that our knowing of the truth is provisional — it's not finished — and it is contingent — it's patterned on Another. Nevertheless, we have foundations for the expressions of truth we give, so far as they are the fruit of a community that lives true to the truth who is Jesus and so far as we have grasped what Jesus the Truth cares about in our world.

And we must not be mistaken; it is just such truth as this that is at stake. Douglas John Hall notes in Dietrich Bonhoeffer's writings, particularly *The Cost of Discipleship*, his impassioned plea "to realize at last that the discipleship of Jesus Christ is a serious business. . . . It is a quest for and a witness to truth in the midst of societies that lie, for authentic goodness in the midst of societies that reward duplicity, for true beauty in the midst of societies that celebrate kitsch and sentimentality."[23] The former dissident and later president of the Czech Republic, Vaclav Havel, points to similar things in his testament to the forces at work in the collapse of Soviet regimes such as Czechoslovakia. There came a time when small acts of de-

---

22. Newbigin, *Foolishness to the Greeks*, p. 59.

23. Douglas John Hall, *The Cross in Our Context: Jesus and the Suffering World* (Minneapolis: Augsburg Fortress, 2003), p. 142.

termination not to believe the lie grew to a groundswell. Duncan Forrester notes that Havel's testament "reminds us of the imperative to speak truth to power, and of the dangers of sloganising rather than offering serious and rigorous theology. It reminds us that theological truth is something to be lived, to be exemplified, rather than just thought and discussed; it is to be lived *together* in the life of the church and in society. And it is a truth that is concrete, challenging and specific rather than general and platitudinous."[24]

Particularity in Discourse

William Lindsey says of prophets that they "always speak perspectively."[25] The postmodern critique of certainty has acquainted us with the fact that this is so of all speech. Cross-cultural missionaries have known it a lot longer! All cognitions of what is true are formed within some society's cultural pattern for thinking and knowing. Even our knowing of the gospel that we understand to be a universally relevant portrait of what is finally and everywhere true comes stated and traditioned in patterns of words and ideas that are a human creation. Lesslie Newbigin put it straightforwardly, in a couple of sentences that are like show-stoppers for many people as they begin to read *Foolishness to the Greeks:* "Neither at the beginning, nor at any subsequent time, is there or can there be a gospel that is not embodied in a culturally conditioned form of words. The idea that one can or could at any time separate out by some process of distillation a pure gospel unadulterated by any cultural accretions is an illusion. It is, in fact, an abandonment of the gospel, for the gospel is about the word made flesh."[26]

Particularist speech is what we have in hand to offer. For many Christians, to be counted as a particular voice speaking from some perspective feels as though their voice is thereby discounted. "Well, that's only your opinion." In reality that is true of all voices, even the ones declaring someone else's particular perspective illegitimate. But that means owning it about ourselves, if we are to have any part in unmasking the pretentions of any others who claim for their own affirmation something that lies beyond

24. Duncan B. Forrester, "The Political Service of Theology in Scotland," in *God in Society: Doing Social Theology in Scotland Today,* ed. William Storrar and Peter Donald (Edinburgh: Saint Andrew Press, 2003), pp. 86-87.

25. William D. Lindsey, "Telling It Slant: American Catholic Public Theology and Prophetic Discourse," *Horizons* 22, no. 1 (1995): 88.

26. Newbigin, *Foolishness to the Greeks,* p. 4.

particularity in some zone of neutrality or objectivity. To hold the posture of those who speak from the place where our own commitments and visions have been formed around this good news of God is to be both more honest and more able to invite others to exhibit similar honesty. At the same time, as Newbigin went on to say, "the gospel, which is from the beginning to the end embodied in culturally conditioned forms, calls into question all cultures, including the one in which it was originally embodied."[27]

To embrace a self-conscious sense of the particularity of our witness challenges the dynamics of discourse that we will find present in many places. The unspoken rules that tend to disenfranchise a particularist voice are also the rules that tend to disallow voices that speak from a number of margins — economic, social, ethnic, etc. And anyone claiming to have a prophetic message calling into question the established wisdom is resisted. William Lindsey addresses "public theology and prophetic discourse" in these terms. Public theology, he says, "implicitly invites questions about the relationship between truth and power in public discourse." To construe that as "civil discourse" in which "all contributors would be required to speak a common 'civil' language," while it sounds generous to all voices, has a resistive and barring effect. "Civil discourse appears on closer inspection to be about something else altogether, and that something else is control of the conversation." It becomes the mechanism for resisting any who claim to be prophets. He concludes that what elicits community resistance to prophetic speech is that "prophets are less preposterous lunatics crying the absurd from the fringes of a society than [they are] people who have managed to invade the center successfully enough to mimic the speech of the center while absolutely refusing the logic that dominates that speech." They are "those who manage to say what is unsayable, against the sheer weight of received truth in socially constructed worlds."[28]

Lindsey borrows from Emily Dickinson to propose that prophecy involves the "ability to tell the truth but tell it slant." Prophetic speech "talks about what those in power talk about but it does so slant and circuitously, opening up the controlled world of the discourse community to an imagination entirely different from the one mandated from on high, and yet so compellingly believable that we wonder why no one has pointed this out to us before."[29]

27. Newbigin, *Foolishness to the Greeks*, p. 4.
28. Lindsey, "Telling It Slant," pp. 89-101.
29. Lindsey, "Telling It Slant," pp. 100-101.

This view of prophetic speech provides the clue that the Christian (prophetic) voice in public discourse must be bilingual. To put it in Newbigin's terms, it must speak both culture and gospel. We speak from within the internal logic of Christian faith and vision among those who share a different internal logic. Knowing and speaking both languages, both logics, is crucial for our communication. At points it means speaking with others in the terms they comprehend and on the ground of logic that makes sense to them. But we will not forever remain merely on that ground, but will give to the discourse the fully particular logic of a community following the lead of Christ. "The goal should not be to replace the language of the liberal cult with that of the Christian cult; rather, it should be to work strenuously at drawing people outside the church into a dialogue that engages their imagination so that they will experience the capacity of Christian truth to illumine the nature of the problems they face and the moral decisions they must make."[30]

Courage in Public Action

Charles West has said that "The church owes the powers of the world a ministry of social imagination."[31] This is not only to be true of our speech and the intellectual imagination that is needed for conceiving social options. It has to do with our action as a Christian community. And that is twofold.

On the one hand, it involves the committed, practiced action of the community to *be* what it espouses. As Newbigin affirms in *Truth to Tell*, "the most important contribution which the church can make to a new social order is to be itself a new social order. More fundamental than any of the things which the church can say or do is the reality of a new society which allows itself to be shaped by the Christian faith."[32] Hauerwas and Willimon say a similar thing: "The church doesn't have a social strategy, the church *is* a social strategy."[33] Or as Hauerwas put it elsewhere: "The church does not have, but rather is a social ethic. That is, she is a social ethic inasmuch as she functions as a criteriological institution — that is, an institution that has

30. Guroian, *Ethics after Christendom*, p. 51.
31. Brownson et al., *StormFront*, p. 101.
32. Newbigin, *Truth to Tell*, p. 85.
33. Hauerwas and Willimon, *Resident Aliens*, p. 43.

learned to embody the form of truth that is charity as revealed in the person and work of Christ."[34]

The Christian community doesn't wait until it can convince the government that a particular practice would be good for society and it becomes formally instituted for the nation. This would be to follow the path of "totalistic reform" against which Ephraim Radner protested many years ago.[35] Instead of that model, by which it looks to the state to implement the moral good, he commends being a "theocratic community" that lives the practices of God whether or not the society as a whole adopts them or legislates them. He sees a difference between the exodus model that looks for an entire reshaping of the social structures and an exilic model in which the community is faithful to *be* the community in allegiance to God while offering its life and vision in service to the empire insofar as the empire may be willing to receive it. The community doesn't wait for the governmental change; it lives it in advance, and does so whether or not the government ever embraces it.

In other words, there is something wrong with the picture when Christians across the country mount, as they did some years ago, a march on Washington to call for the government to do something about homelessness in America. We should wonder how many of the hundreds of thousands who appeared had themselves given shelter to any homeless persons in their spare bedrooms or in the largely unused basements of their church facilities. In such a scenario, the government becomes a kind of mechanism for the church to use to fulfill its ethical vision. That forfeits its own calling to be the witnessing agent of the kind of world God intends and brings — whatever the government does.

Several years ago, I discovered among people in the Dutch Reformed Churches of South Africa that they have experienced in a few short years since 1994 the reverse image of this. They have had the protective moral covering removed, and they find themselves lacking the capacity to deal with ethical choices. Many such choices had previously been pre-made for them by the government, but that is no longer true. Now they must make them, but will need to gain the skills of moral discernment to do so. If they gain those skills, the "freedom" that has left them feeling naked and ex-

34. Stanley Hauerwas, *Truthfulness and Tragedy* (Notre Dame: Notre Dame University Press, 1977), pp. 142-43.

35. Ephraim Radner, "From 'Liberation' to 'Exile': A New Image for Church Mission," *Christian Century* 106 (18 October 1989): 931-34.

posed may turn out to be a truer freedom, one that clothes them in a new kind of community!

On the other hand, the rationale for the church *as* social strategy means that there *will* and *must* be intentionality about how it observes, discerns, and acts in its public locations. It will be a community that lives beyond itself. This is the thrust of Raymond Fung's choice to put working at the Isaiah agenda first in the logical order of his three-fold vision, even if it is not always so chronologically.

Here the notion of "public theologizing" may appear to reach its limits, if it only means conversation and discourse in the public arena. Of course, even speech is sometimes more than mere conversation and is a dangerous act of resistance or defiance. Better, though, that public theologizing be construed actively as the argument or imagination made with hands instead of voices. This is particularly true when it comes to solidarity with the poor or marginalized or crushed. Solidarity is a tangible, lived experience of walking alongside, not just saying so. Solidarity cannot avoid the touch of deeds.

In 1991, the Western Theological Seminary community (in Holland, Michigan) came face to face with some important information, and with it, a challenge to act. While there was considerable denial about it around town, there were in fact people going hungry with insufficient food or financial resources. Right at that time, the state government took measures to cut back its program of general assistance by one third, meaning that many people who before had barely made ends meet would no longer be able to do so. Many with mental disabilities were being de-institutionalized, and that further pressured the resources of local agencies. Led by students, and joined by faculty, the seminary offered its kitchen and commons area and in partnership with a local agency began serving a free hot noon meal every weekday. Volunteers from over twenty churches and food donations from local businesses and individuals have sustained the effort. It continues to be a place where the hospitality of a shared meal joins people across wide diversities in culture, language, education, employment, and economic status.

It was widely thought at the time the seminary made this response that the government's budgetary action was really intended to encourage people on state aid to move away from the state and become someone else's problem. A noon meal may have made the difference and thwarted that intent for some of the folks who became the seminary's noon-meal friends. It was a quiet argument, but one with substance.

In all of this there is risk. "The public square will be a place of conflict where one can be wounded. . . . To claim that the Gospel is public truth is to enter into a struggle in which we can expect to be wounded. But these wounds are the authenticating marks of the missionary church."[36] *The* mark, par excellence, Douglas John Hall would add.[37]

An Eye on the Horizon

I am very fascinated with flying. I gather from those who know the art that what is called the "attitude" of a plane is its position relative to three axes. It includes bank or roll, the raising or lowering of the wings in relation to the fuselage. It includes pitch, the upward or downward direction in which the nose is pointed. It includes yaw, the left or right directions in which the nose is pointed. (That one is *really* important if there's a crosswind! If a plane is aimed directly toward a particular destination, and there is a twenty-mile-per-hour crosswind, the plane will never arrive at its intended destination. It must direct the angle of its flight sufficiently into the wind so that the angle of its flight and the force of the wind work together to bring it to the intended destination.) This image may be suggestive for the matter of posture. In what direction, with what tilt are we positioned in our public engagements? What is our *attitude?*

There's one more important feature to a plane's attitude. Its position, its bank and pitch and yaw, are gauged in relationship to the horizon! Our voice and posture in public theologizing are oriented to the horizon of the coming reign of God. The horizon is important if we are to avoid the twin dangers of thinking that we build the kingdom of God on earth (and that can be the vision of the right as well as the left, as we are discovering!) or thinking that we have no responsibility to act toward what the kingdom of God promises. We need to think neither too much nor too little of our efforts. "While Christians ought not to expect the advent of a new Christian society," says Vigen Guroian, "their presence in this society as a dialogic community of memory and tradition nonetheless makes possible practical embodiments of the Christian faith even within secular institutions."[38]

We will keep focus and maintain our *attitude* by keeping an eye to the

36. Lesslie Newbigin, "The Gospel and Our Culture: The Gospel as Public Truth." Documents of a National Consultation, the Hayes, Swanwick, 11-17 July 1992 (Swanwick, UK: British and Foreign Bible Society, 1992).

37. Hall, *The Cross in Our Context*, pp. 137ff.

38. Guroian, *Ethics after Christendom*, p. 48.

horizon, hoping ultimately in the promises of God rather than our own actions or those of other forces. On the horizon, what we see indelibly printed there are the tears of the cross and the joy of resurrection. And therefore, *hope* is there. In the daily exercise of the church's public theologizing, it is this hope that will

- guide action and strategy
- critique agendas and means
- redefine success
- identify idols
- qualify our best achievements as proximate practical embodiments
- give caution about imagined finalities
- give criteria for rejoicing!

These are the tokens of what is coming!

Cultivating Ways of Christ

1998

With the publication in 1986 of his book *Foolishness to the Greeks*, Lesslie Newbigin set loose in the United States a new wave of influence among pastoral leaders. For decades, his influence had already molded the way people thought about an important range of issues. His missionary view of the nature of the church *(The Household of God)* and his insistence on the pursuit of its visible unity *(Is Christ Divided?)* had taught us how to think about the church. He had led us to reckon with theological underpinnings for the mission of the church *(The Relevance of Trinitarian Doctrine for Today's Mission, The Open Secret, Mission in Christ's Way)*. He had engaged the relationship of Christian faith to the variety of other religious faiths in the world *(A Faith for This One World?, The Finality of Christ)*. He had displayed in it all a deeply pastoral style, whether in the villages of India or the bureaucratic halls of Europe *(A South India Diary, The Good Shepherd)*. We looked over his shoulder as he did the work of an evangelist among children of the traditions of the West as well as the East *(Honest Religion for Secular Man,* and the lesser known but very significant *Christ Our Eternal Contemporary)*.[1]

But now he had turned his gaze in a new direction. It was not divorced from all the issues he had dealt with for years, so productively for so many people. In fact, it was a pointed application of that missionary angle of vision, now turning it upon the Western culture which was his own cul-

---

1. Publication details for these and others of Newbigin's writings are available online at www.newbigin.net. The comprehensive bibliographic database on the site is fully searchable, and many of the texts themselves are freely available in digital form.

ture of origin and now his context in retirement. What he asked seemed rude to some, incomprehensible to many, but liberating to still others. He wondered what a genuine missionary encounter of the gospel with Western culture would be like if the encounter were to take its cue from centuries of missionary experience, from the recently recovered sense of the church's essential missionary identity, and from the insights of companion churches around the globe which were the fruit of the missionary approach of Western churches. Whatever had been true of the comfort of churches in their Western, Christianized societies in the past had now vanished, and the time was more than ripe for the question. With *Foolishness to the Greeks* and numerous other books and articles and addresses, he has made this the orienting issue for a generation of emerging leadership in churches in the United States and other Western societies.

That alone has made him an indispensable resource for pastoral leadership in general and for the practice of preaching in particular. Under that vision, you can't preach the same any more. It is not the same as preaching sermons among church membership and a general citizenry that come to the preaching to be nourished in the moral and spiritual character assumed to be the norms of a Christian society. In a mission context, and in a missional church, the requirements for the biblical nourishment of the community and the clear articulation of liberating news in multiple spheres of human living are not just raised to a new level, they make of preaching something different. In an atmosphere where it is no longer true that all good people are *supposed to* believe (i.e., they *ought to*, and it may be presumed that deep down they already do), preaching can bolster little of what is socially expected, and instead it invites, welcomes, and enables people to believe things that are odd compared to the going versions of reality. It participates in the inner dialogue between the gospel and the assumptions of one's own culture and cultivates a community for whom continuing conversion is its habitual approach. It is for the art of that sort of preaching that Newbigin provides essential resources for the preacher.

In reflections on the significance of Newbigin's work just after his death in January 1998, I found myself referring to him as an "apostle of faith and witness."[2] I never was around Bishop Newbigin when he was not working hard to cultivate for the church a sense of its authority to preach the gospel, and its authority to believe that it is true. In deep response to the

---

2. George R. Hunsberger, "Apostle of Faith and Witness," *The Gospel and Our Culture Newsletter,* special edition (April 1998): 2.

crisis of missional nerve in the churches of the West, which had become ultimately a crisis of faith, he seemed to have been called to be pastor to us all. That pastoral quality was much in evidence from the beginning of his ministry as bishop in the Church of South India and throughout his years in India. But, no less, he pastored us in the churches of the West. He gave us ways to believe, whether under the privatizing effects of modernity or the pluralist social arrangements of postmodernity. In our progress-and-success culture, he helped us see that death finally mocks all our greatest achievements, and our only hope lies in the risen Christ, not in the permanence of our accomplishments.

In the latter years of his life, it was Newbigin's purpose to open Western culture to a missionary dialogue with the gospel. In the course of that effort, he was essentially cultivating ways of Christ for people living in the midst of the cultural transition from modern to postmodern and in what had already become a post-Christian social era. His cultivation of ways of believing, of witnessing, of being community, and of living in hope anticipates the daily and weekly preoccupations of any preacher sensitive to the demands of the present day. For these crucial elements of a preacher's vocation today, important resources are to be found in Newbigin's approach.

Ways of Belief

When Christians feel intimidated about telling other people the Christian message, it is not just a matter of believing that people will not like being told that this is true and other claims to truth are called into question by it. It goes much deeper, to the ability to believe it themselves in a world that tells them, in one way or another, that a religious conviction cannot lay claim to be the truth in any factual sense and must be held only as a private option. The strict dichotomy that grew up under Enlightenment rationality between knowable public fact and chosen private opinion already pushed in this direction. The emerging postmodern sense that all knowing is from some particular perspective further relativized all claims to truth and questioned such claims as exertions of the will to power. Christians imagining any form of direct public assertion of the Christian message do not have to be told that it will meet with a cloud of questions about its legitimacy. Besides pushing them toward silence, the atmosphere erodes the strength of their own inner conviction that the Bible's account of things can be taken to be a valid option for construing the world.

Newbigin always wrestled with such matters himself, and the way he found pathways through the intimidating terrain lays foundations for others. His early theological training under John Oman of Cambridge had taught him the importance of recognizing the personhood of God, and that God's personal character is displayed by the freedom to act, and to choose the time and place of such action. God can be known in the ways that any person can be known, by what that person reveals in the choices made and actions taken. This sense of the necessity of revelation as the way to know God had come to be viewed by many, under the imprint of the Enlightenment's confidence in autonomous human reason, as a less sure form of knowledge than that gained through the scientific method and the certainty of tracing cause and effect. What Newbigin ultimately discerned, helped immeasurably by the work of Michael Polanyi, was that science was as much a tradition, borne by a community and rooted in certain beliefs, as is any religious tradition, including that of the church. Polanyi's book *Personal Knowledge* gave clarity to Newbigin's sense that knowing what the gospel announces and knowing what science detects are not so fundamentally different sorts of knowing as the culture tends to assume.[3] In fact, Newbigin shows that Christian faith is not irrational but represents a wider rationality than the norms of scientific discovery posit, because the gospel opens the question of purpose which scientific knowing set aside in favor of cause and effect.[4]

Newbigin's use of Polanyi's approach, most emphatically in the first five chapters of *The Gospel in a Pluralist Society,* provides an apologetic approach that undergirds the faith of believing people, something that is essential for the presence of confident witness.[5] I have watched as students have read those sixty-five pages and found themselves liberated to believe — to really believe — that this good news is true and can be told with assurance. The preacher today is in the business of securing ways for people to see how they can believe. What I have called elsewhere Newbigin's "postmodern apologetic" is a helpful frame of reference for the preacher's work.[6] It is essential for a context where Christian faith is no longer merely what polite citizens are expected to believe.

3. Michael Polanyi, *Personal Knowledge: Towards a Post-Critical Philosophy* (Chicago: University of Chicago Press, 1958).

4. See Newbigin's argument to this effect in chapter 3 of *Foolishness to the Greeks: The Gospel and Western Culture* (Grand Rapids: Eerdmans, 1986).

5. Lesslie Newbigin, *The Gospel in a Pluralist Society* (Grand Rapids: Eerdmans, 1989).

6. See above, pp. 16-20.

Ways of Witness

Postmodern people have a way of using qualifying phrases that show a sensitivity to the opinions of others. Affirmations are prefaced by phrases like "It seems to me," or "I believe that . . . ," or "I have found this to be true for me." The language is generous and tolerant. But somewhere in it there lurks the potential that all notions are held as true only "for me," with little or nothing presumed to be true also for others. Newbigin helps us see that even within the generous tolerance of humility about the provisional character of all our knowing there is nonetheless the possibility — for all postmodern people on all sorts of issues — to hold some things with *universal intent,* that is, as being true for everyone, however partial may be our grasp of it. Such is surely the sense Christian believers get about how the gospel they read about in the New Testament expects to be believed. It is announced there with the firm conviction that this good news is for and about the whole world, not just a particular few within it. Jesus' prophetic utterance, "You shall be my witnesses," both energizes them with a sense of their calling and haunts them with the dilemmas it causes in the midst of the postmodern mood. It is not hard to see how deliberate, direct Christian witness rubs against the sensibilities of a world living on the backside of several centuries of Western colonialism. What right do Christians have to pretend to be the bearers of a message everyone should believe?

It is to this matter of "the duty and authority of the church to preach the gospel" that Newbigin has constantly addressed himself in an attempt to build confidence for Christian witness.[7] What is most distinctive about his rationale for witness in the contemporary world is that it is grounded in particularity, not undone by it. Most take the particularity of the Christian church and its historic cultural location primarily in the West to be the problem that thwarts any possibility of universal witness (whether that means among all peoples of the world or all people in our own locale). If only some point of reference in a universally validated gospel could be found, then, it is supposed, witness could rest on that ground. Some seek that under the rubric of objective truth, others in universally demonstrable

7. See the article Newbigin published by this title in the materials of the convening assembly of the World Council of Churches, "The Duty and Authority of the Church to Preach the Gospel," *The Church's Witness to God's Design,* Amsterdam Assembly Series, vol. 2 (New York: Harper and Brothers, 1948), pp. 19-35.

religious principles. In either case, the particularity of the church is suspect and believed to interfere with a justification for witness.

But not so for Newbigin. The rationale for witness, for the mission of the church and thus its very existence, does not lie in some universal principle distilled out from the particularity of Christian communities, but is rooted precisely in their particularity! He finds it an unworkable myth that we could only witness forthrightly if we somehow could rise above and beyond particularized belief to some universal knowledge. That is impossible, at any rate. But what is more important still, for Newbigin, is that he finds in the biblical rationale for witness the notion that a true particular faith is exactly where the universal scope of witness finds its grounding. He shows this in what he calls the "logic of election."[8] In his understanding of the "missionary significance of the biblical doctrine of election" we find a thread that runs through his major work on mission theology, *The Open Secret,* and in fact throughout the range of his writings.[9] By the term *election* Newbigin refers to God's choice of Israel to be God's particular people, to be blessed by God and to be a blessing to the nations, and God's choice of the incipient church, the earliest circle of disciples, to be witnesses to the life, teaching, death, and resurrection of Jesus. In both cases, the choice of the nation and the church is the choice of a particular community to be the means by which people of other particularities will hear and see the witness. In the very act of witness from one particularity to another, and in the birthing of faith in persons and communities to whom the witness is born, the healing reconciliation about which the gospel speaks is coming about. In the end, so declares Paul in Romans 9–11, both the Jew and the Greek are dependent on the witness of the "other" from whom the gospel is received. God's method of choosing particular witnesses is congruent with the social nature of the gospel which envisions the healing of the nations.

The consequence of such a rationale as this for the church's mission of witness is an attitude of humility. Any missionary who recognizes this as the source of authority for commending the gospel with *universal intent* will commend it knowing that the particularity of the missionary church's

8. Newbigin, *The Gospel in a Pluralist Society,* chap. 7.

9. Lesslie Newbigin, *The Open Secret: Sketches for a Missionary Theology* (Grand Rapids: Eerdmans, 1978 [rev. ed. 1995]). For an extended treatment of Newbigin's way of seeing the biblical doctrine of election as the key to a rationale for mission and for a theology of cultural plurality, see George R. Hunsberger, *Bearing the Witness of the Spirit: Lesslie Newbigin's Theology of Cultural Plurality* (Grand Rapids: Eerdmans, 1998), especially chaps. 2 and 3.

faith must be worn with confidence but not assumed to be absolute or final. The conviction with which the gospel is told leads to a humble form of missionary dialogue with the ways that a new person or community or culture grasps and exhibits the gospel in response to the Spirit.

Preaching that approaches its task in this way will model the sense that in any preaching — in sermon, conversation, demonstration, or deed — the calling of the church is to give the gospel away and expect wonderful new flowerings of its expression in the recipients of the message. Confident witness by the whole community is nourished best when that is the case.

Ways of Community

If Newbigin has been an apostle of faith and witness, he has always been an apostle on behalf of the church. It is the church's faith, the church's witness, that he is concerned to nourish. Christian existence is fundamentally corporate, and Christian calling is a corporately shared calling. While not denying the individuality of each person's experience of Christ, he warns against the individualism of belief and identity that so strongly shapes Western forms of Christian life and cuts short the corporate nature of God's salvation. For Newbigin, the church is the chosen witness that bears in word and deed the witness of the Spirit.

This theme has always been a strong one in Newbigin's thought. He presents it with special relevance in his most recent writings and thus helps to form a postmodern, post-Christendom way to understand that the very existence of the church as a community of Christ and the character of its life together are already critical features of its whole witness to Christ and the reign of God he announced. The church is the "sign, instrument, and foretaste" of the reign of God, he so often has said. It is the firstfruits of the new creation in the Spirit.

His stress in later years on understanding the congregation to be a "hermeneutic of the gospel" forms an important answer to another of the authority questions postmodern people have, "Why the church?" By what authority, and on what ground, is there a rationale for the church to exist at all?[10] The authority to witness is its authority to exist: the only adequate witness is one that iterates what is visibly and truly embodied in a community

10. Newbigin, *The Gospel in a Pluralist Society,* chap. 18.

of people embraced by the message. The presence of the Christian community functions as a hermeneutical key, an interpretive lens through which onlookers gain a view of the gospel in the living colors of common life. The Christian congregation offers itself to be a community within which one can grow into faith in the gospel, put on the garb of its followers, and join oneself to the distinctive practices that mark the community as God's own people.

This is refreshing good news in light of the identity crisis which has seized so many churches in these days beyond a churched culture. In an earlier day, it could be assumed what a church is for. It served the chaplaincy needs of a Christianized civic order. But that day has been passing away. Churches can still seem to thrive by providing for the populace the religious goods and services it seeks. But even in that role the church finds uneasiness. What are we for, when stripped of those things that used to give us meaning?

Both the content of what is preached and the manner in which preaching addresses the Christian community week after week are crucial for the recovery of the church's identity. Preaching first has to know that it shapes communal identity, for good or for ill. Then it has to wrestle with what sense of identity has faithful roots in the gospel and rebirths the church's reason to exist in the present circumstances in the United States. Finally, it has to discover what posture of preaching cultivates such identity. For all these, the vision Newbigin has for the church's vocation is an invaluable resource.

Ways of Hope

Another aspect of the humility which Newbigin both espouses and models lies in his sense that in the final analysis death mocks all our achievements. Hope for the future must rather be found in the distinctive way the Christian faith is rooted in history. The gospel comes in the form of a narrative that renders accessible to us the character, actions, and purposes of God. The particular actions of God told in the narrative are world news, not just news for the religion page. The narrative claims that no less than the meaning of the world's life is revealed in the story whose center is Jesus Christ. His heralding of the coming reign of God shows the meaning of the story by showing its end!

Hope is not convincingly cultivated in a congregation by preaching that hope resides in the success of our efforts and the height of our achievements. Biblical visions of hope are not lodged in the actions of savvy entrepreneurs but in the actions of God against all odds. The coming reign of

God that is hoped for is not portrayed in the Bible as the cumulative effect of human efforts but as God's gracious gift. Faithful preaching invites us to receive it and enter it, not try to build it.

There are deep pastoral implications if we see things this way. I remember the first time I personally encountered the impact of Newbigin's vision and the way it nourished me at a time of exhaustion and grief in the work of pastoral ministry. It was in 1980. I had just returned from an intense year of work in Kenya, working among Ugandan refugees from Idi Amin's regime. Now back in the United States, a friend commended *The Open Secret* to me and I began to read it.

At about the same time, contact with people in the congregation I had pastored until a year and a half before made me aware that serious fracture lines were emerging in the congregation, and its unity and continued existence were threatened. I did not yet know that before long my worst fears would be realized. A division would leave a fragile remnant behind that would try for several more years to rebuild the community. But eventually it was to end in the dissolution of the congregation.

I came to the place in the book where Newbigin observed that all our greatest achievements are destined to go down into the chasm of death and become part of the rubble of history. Or, if they should remain at the time of Christ's return, they will be subject to God's discriminating judgment. Ultimately, he said, our hope lies not in the quality or permanence of our achievements but in Christ who has passed through the chasm of death and come up on the other side in his resurrection. The significance of our work is not in its success or achievement but in its relationship to the risen Lord.

This redirection of hope nourished me in the midst of my fears for the congregation I had been a part of for over five years. A few years later it would console me again when the news of its death would overwhelm me with grief.

The cultivation of hope lodged in its proper place, in Christ, is desperately needed in churches and preachers living in today's success-and-achievement world. Newbigin's help nourishes the kind of hope that overwhelms the world's despair and releases the demands for performance as the basis for self-worth. It fashions preachers and pastoral leaders whose confidence is as deep as the resurrection of Christ is sure.

Index of Subjects and Names

Abraham, William, 93n.14, 95n.15
Ammerman, Nancy, 39-40
Apologetics: ecclesial failure, 32; post-modern apologetic (Newbigin), 11, 16-18, 26, 154-56; proper confidence, 143-44; true to the truth, 79-82, 144; "wider rationality," 16, 18, 23, 26, 28, 155. *See also* Newbigin, Lesslie; Po-lanyi, Michael
Arias, Mortimer, 56-58, 91, 93n.14

Barrett, Lois, 110n.
Bearing the Witness of the Spirit, 98n.16, 157n.9, 13n.4
Bockmuehl, Klaus, 114
Boer, Harry, 91
Bonhoeffer, Dietrich, 144
Bosch, David, 34, 45-47, 76, 89-90
Brownson, James, 2n.1. *See also* *StormFront*

Carey, William, 89
Callahan, Kennon, 21, 86n.1
Charisms, 131
Christendom: clericalism and pas-toral formation, 20, 78-79; post-Christendom ecclesial imagination, 19, 44-45, 73-75, 86, 102, 158; privileged status gone, 11, 20-24, 83, 134; residual impact on ecclesiology, 16, 45-46, 57-59, 83-85
Church: body of people sent, 34, 46; community of the reign of God, 67-68; congregation and denomination, 38-40; ecclesial identity crisis, 21-23, 30-33, 43-45, 74-75; embodiment of the gospel, 26-27, 39-40, 82-83, 99-100; ex-ilic model, 22-23, 22n.24; hermeneutic of the gospel, 14, 82, 99-100, 142, 158-59; local vocation, 110-32; marks of the church, 45-49; missionary by its very nature, 18-20, 46-49, 73, 82-83; origination in the gospel, 51-52, 62-63; "parallel" community, 85; public assembly, 135-36; recovery of voice and identity, 139-41; reign of God, relation to, 20, 62-65; sign and foretaste, 64-66; "theocratic" community, 148; truly community, 76-79; vendor of religious goods and services, 33-37, 49-51, 76-77, 128
Clements, Keith, 139
Conversion: church as fruit of, 83; con-tinual, 52, 95, 115, 141-42, 153; defined, 15-16; diverse forms of, 96; gift of the Spirit, 70; gospel-culture encounter, 13-15, 104, 107
Corporate discernment, 118-23

Index of Scripture References